MW00981607

I could not put this book down. After each chapter I found myself asking What's next? How will God show up? What will Jenny say next? The world needs more books like this. Honest, transparent, authentic, vulnerable, and human are only a few of the adjectives that come to mind. Faith can almost seem sterile or vanilla in our day and age but Jenny brings a freshness to show how faith is to be lived out. She doesn't claim to have it all together, but she is committed to the process of integrating her relationship with Christ into every aspect of her life. You will be surprised, entertained, and probably cringe at times, but my prayer is that you will be inspired to explore the intricacies of faith regardless of your place on the journey.

—*Rev Guy Scholz;*
three-time bestselling author;
veteran church planter and social worker;
splits his time between Calgary, AB and Nashville, TN

"When I started reading this book, I had real trouble putting it down. The author does a masterful job of bringing us into her life. You will feel like you are right there with her as she writes about her years as a young Hutterite girl on the Pine Creek colony. You will see God at work in her life as a teenager, a mom, and a wife. At times my eyes watered with tears. At other times I found myself laughing. At all times I knew I had been invited into a story of God's grace and kindness."

John Drisner,
District Superintendent,
Saskatchewan Pentecostal Assemblies of Canada;
Lead Pastor, The Neighbourhood Church, Saskatoon

"*I Met Jesus at the Gym* is an authentic story that had us laughing one minute and teary-eyed the next. From cringing to rejoicing, this will refresh your soul as you enjoy the warmth of God's grace. This book gives a beautiful glimpse into the Hutterite culture. For the curious reader, this is one of those stories you don't want to see end."

Lance and Cindy Steeves,
Pastors at Cold Lake Community Church

"A must read for anyone struggling through life's problems, huge or small. A show of how faith, courage and love can get one through the hardest of times."

Darrell Wright NHC, NHE

To Theresa.
So sweet to finally meet you again Larry ♥ od you both
Jenny.

I Met
JESUS
at the
GYM

Jenny Rumancik

I MET JESUS AT THE GYM
Copyright © 2016 by Jenny Rumancik

All rights reserved. Neither this publication nor any part of this publication may be reproduced or transmitted in any form or by any means, electronic or mechanical, including photocopying, recording or any information storage and retrieval system, without permission in writing from the author.

Scripture taken from the Holy Bible, NEW INTERNATIONAL VERSION®. Copyright © 1973, 1978, 1984, 2011 by Biblica, Inc. All rights reserved worldwide. Used by permission. NEW INTERNATIONAL VERSION® and NIV® are registered trademarks of Biblica, Inc. Use of either trademark for the offering of goods or services requires the prior written consent of Biblica US, Inc. • Scripture quotations are taken from the Holy Bible, New Living Translation, copyright ©1996, 2004, 2007 by Tyndale House Foundation. Used by permission of Tyndale House Publishers, Inc., Carol Stream, Illinois 60188. All rights reserved. • Scripture quotations marked KJV are taken from the Holy Bible, King James Version, which is in the public domain.

Printed in Canada

ISBN: 978-1-4866-1112-6

Word Alive Press
131 Cordite Road, Winnipeg, MB R3W 1S1
www.wordalivepress.ca

WORD ALIVE
—P R E S S—

MIX
Paper from
responsible sources
FSC
www.fsc.org   FSC® C016245

Library and Archives Canada Cataloguing in Publication

Rumancik, Jenny, 1976-, author
      I met Jesus at the gym / Jenny Rumancik.

Issued in print and electronic formats.
ISBN 978-1-4866-1112-6 (paperback).--ISBN 978-1-4866-111-33 (pdf).--
ISBN 978-1-4866-1114-0 (html).--ISBN 978-1-4866-1115-7 (epub)

      1. Rumancik, Jenny, 1976-. 2. God (Christianity)--Faithfulness.
3. Christian life. I. Title.

BV4501.3.R84 2015   248.4   C2015-907502-5
                                                  C2015-907503-3

DEDICATION

I DEDICATE THIS WRITING JOURNEY TO YOU MY SWEET BABY GIRL, AUBREE DAWN, MY beloved, late grandaughter. You came into our life and proved that every baby is truly a blessing sent from above. You may have only been in our lives for a short while but in that time you proved how great, and all powerful our God really is. Because you were born with an inoperable heart defect, we were only supposed to have you for a few days. In your short little life, your sweet smile affected many people and your life was well seen as a miracle. You taught me that Grandma needs to focus only on what's most important, that true validation only comes through the Lord Jesus Christ, and that what He thinks of me is most important. It was a privilege to be your grandma. I watched you transform your mommy and daddy into two courageous young people, and I am blessed to have your mother in our family. Both of you have taught me that everyone comes into your life for a season and a reason. I love you, sweet baby girl, and can't wait to see you in heaven one precious day.

Love,
Grandma

ACKNOWLEDGEMENTS

WHAT A JOURNEY WRITING THIS BOOK HAS BEEN! I CAN TRULY SAY I HAD THE TIME OF my life! Thank you to Women's Journey of Faith and Word Alive Press for giving me the pathway to succeed in my writing dream. My season working with the Word Alive Press team and my editor, Susan Fish, has been an exhilarating ride. Susan, you have proven to me that editors rock! Your God-given gift in critiquing a written work while keeping the author's voice intact proved flawless. I appreciated your quote: it takes two people to write a book, one to write the story and the other to rip it out of her hand when it's time. I will never forget the day when you kindly had to rip it out of my hand. Thank you for your professionalism that at times turned to friendship.   Kylee Unrau, my Project Manager, thank you for always being there to answer my many questions. Your advice always helped me understand my writing path. I think you nailed many of my hard days by simply asking "Jenny, who is your target audience?" That has to be the best writer's question ever! Your expertise in the writing journey was truly appreciated.

Thank you to Dora Maendel: this story brought with it a lot of unexpected emotions and I will never forget the hard days where you reached through the phone lines and nourished my lonely heart with your kind words. Thank you for the wise counsel; you are a true writer and I respect you greatly. Piecing together the Hutterite culture within my story was no easy task and I am so thankful for the day I found the Hutterite Brethren website. The written information was a fountain of refreshing work and made me very proud to have lived in such a culture.

Guy Scholz: Thank you for reading my manuscript and helping me with the priceless job of writing my back cover. Your creativity mixed with experience came at the most perfect time. Once again God proved that all I needed was at hand.

My Aunt Barbara: I remember the warmth of our visit at the beginning of this writing project. I sat and listened as you reminisced about the beginning years of Pinecreek and enjoyed the picture you painted in my mind. I loved how excited you were for me, and felt like my Dad would have shared your same sense of enthusiasm.

Beth Moore: Your Bible studies have enriched my faith walk. I thank God for your gift of bringing biblical theology to a hungry generation of woman. The majority of my writing days were started with me, you, and James. I was immersed in your study of the book of James, Mercy Triumphs. What a perfect Bible study to do while writing about family. Your homework study guide was such a tremendous tool in allowing the Holy Spirit to guide my fingers on the keys of my laptop. This Bible Study turned out to be the perfect book plan. Thank you, Beth Moore. You rock!

Thank you to all my coworkers, my cheering crew at work for always listening to all my little tidbits. Your excited voices kept me believing this book could be possible.

My Bible study ladies and church family: Your enthusiasm was mixed with both prayers and support. Thank you for making me feel like I was set apart for God's greatness.

To my in-laws: Thank you for helping me with the responsibilities on the home front and helping me get some much-needed, uninterrupted writing weeks. Even though my father-in-law Larry Rumancik left this world before this book could be finished, I will never forget the supportive part he played. As I was crying late one night, my dreams soon welcomed a gift from above: I saw my father-in-law, pen and paper in hand, sitting quietly at a table. I called his name but he did not lift his attentive eye away from the papers he was holding. When he finally was through, he turned to me and said confidently "There—is this kind you would like?" My spirit leapt, for I realized it was a writing catalogue. His glasses perched on the lower end of his nose as his kind eyes met mine. I loved it! It was then I knew you were marketing my project from up above...I love you, Papa, and miss you dearly. Thank you!

I would like to thank my mother-in-law for being involved in all the small details of finalizing a writing project. Believe it or not, I value your attention to small important details. Thank you for your willingness to cheer me on to the finish line while running some of the race with me. We truly are becoming the biblical Ruth and Naomi.

Also, thanks to my mother for being there for me even when the road seemed scary. You allowed me to wade into the stormy seas of our family story. You protected me from writing down the wrong path. You listened to the hard parts and helped me get them just right. Thank you for your courage and for your blessing to write this story. I will always remember that it was you and I that laughed at some of the story lines in the rough draft. I am proud to be your daughter and thankful for the things you have taught me. You set a bar that at times it seems too high to reach. My mother is the Proverbs 31 woman!

To my hot husband: You are the reason this writing project took flight. You celebrated my title and talent and became my biggest fan. I love you and thank you for encouraging me to go for it! Everyone needs a book manager who is as supportive as you've been. The hours you spent proofreading our story was a challenge and I felt loved all the while. You have blessed me with your courage as I wrote our story for the entire world to see so that people could be blessed by what God can do. I love how you have made me feel that I had the best story of all. Thank you for investing in me and holding my hand while I pressed the submit button.

To my two sons, Bailey and Glen, and two daughters, Sadie and Emma, for letting Mom spend all those hours writing. You really are the best cheering crew ever. Mom loves you very much. Sadie I am so proud of the little mom you became. You found your independence and I am so proud of you.

To Jesus: My best friend, my Saviour, my co-author. You promised that so much blessing would come of this situation. I sit in awe of your fulfillment to that promise. You have never left my side. Thank you. You have given me all that I have needed. No more and no less of exactly all it took to complete this writing journey. I have enjoyed growing in You and shrinking in self. Thank you for loving me, for choosing me for this specific destiny. I can't wait to see the blessings that will come of this writing project. I LOVE YOU, LORD!

FOREWORD

LIVING OUT AN AUTHENTIC FAITH IS MESSY. IT INVOLVES RELATIONSHIPS AND expectations that are flawed in one way or another. These tend to chip away at our identity in Christ. And we've all been there and seen parts of our lives crumble from the weight of hard times and hard reality. Maybe not all of us have reached rock bottom, but most of us have at least come close to the jagged-edged pit of dark, lonely, brokenness. And yet that too is part of living out an authentic faith and need not be suppressed in our memories as if it all were make-believe.

Thankfully, Jenny doesn't pretend in her faith. She met Jesus at the gym as well as many other places in her journey. I've known the Rumancik family for close to six years. They have been a wonderful blessing to myself, my family, and our church. Here Jenny tells her story, which is wrapped tight in relationships and expectations, the two often being at odds with one another. Yet, through all adversity and strife, Jenny's faith echoes off cavern walls in a distinct and known way. She, like you and me, holds on to Jesus as He reveals His presence in her life. And best of all, He does so amidst authentic brokenness.

As a pastor, I have been blessed with countless stories from Christians. They too were challenged in their faith in real ways. This is not a book on different worldviews, though their troubles also are real. Rather, it's Jenny's story about actual interactions, celebrations, challenges, and divine appointments. For those who may struggle with the notion of the supernatural, I would say to give Jenny's book a read. Her encounters with the living Christ can bring all of us hope as we battle the daily grind.

There is also a sense of rural history within these pages. Most do not know anything about the Hutterites, and Jenny brings to life some of their cultural ways. Her being a former Hutterite helps flesh scenes out that are alien to us. It also reminds that there is diversity within the faith. Not all express Christianity in the same manner, but all who call themselves Christians still express Christ.

Jenny's honesty in both the challenges and celebrations encourages us to interact with our faith in a real way. However, her words are not merely about yesterday's events, for she truly looks to follow our Lord in all aspects of her life. When you spend time with her and her family, you find that discussion often turn to what God is doing amidst work, school, friendships, and everything else in between. Her story is a reflection of her life and a host of memories of the journey that she continues to venture into with her family. It is an authentic retelling of the things that tend to drive us away from God, yet through the infinite wisdom and providence of the Lord, pushed Jenny into a deeper and stronger relationship with Christ. For that is what the faith is truly made of. Doctrine and theology has a place and an importance of course, but knowing about the Lord and knowing the Lord are as different as seeing briefly the reflection of a loved one in store windows on a busy December street as opposed to sitting across from that someone with a cup of coffee in a warm cafe.

As you read Jenny's story, know that Jesus is always within reach. No matter the difficulties that you face, nor the trouble that lurks around future's corner, Jesus can be met anywhere, even at a gym.

—Reverend Aaron Talbot
Pastor, Church of God,
Churchbridge, SK

PREFACE

I decided that I would go to the only place I found comfort: the gym. We had a beautiful new facility with an indoor soccer field and an upper level walking track and, of course, a spacious workout area. I found myself at the gym with a fresh Timmies coffee in one hand, and my Bible and journal in the other. As I laced up my running shoes, I could feel the pressures building. I shrugged off the tears stinging the corner of my eyes and took a deep breath. I would find the strength to survive another day. As I began to walk the track, I began to pray, asking God to please help me endure the pain of my breaking heart and the cruel thoughts constantly telling me that I was a hopeless cause. I didn't make it around the first loop before I felt the strongest sense that I was not alone. As I looked around, it was clear that I was the only one on the walking track and on the third floor. I felt a strong sense of peace and warmth flood my soul and began to pray even more intimately. I can not recall my exact words but I do remember the desperate plea that came out of my being when my tears poured afresh and faith turned to cold fear. "Lord, why this? Why did this have to happen? I don't understand all of this. It's too much, I can't bear the pain." As my emotions erupted in uncontrollable sobs, I heard Him as clear as ever. He spoke right to my heart. It wasn't an audible voice but a still small voice just like it states in Scripture. His voice echoed with tenderness and compassion and I will never forget his words: "Jenny, I need you to heal and in order for you to do this I had to take your biggest distraction away." I was overcome with His response. It was clear and precise and I was in awe. As I allowed all the fears to melt away, I began to believe in what He had said. With Jesus by my side, I walked and jogged my way around the track. He had never left me. He was there now, right there with me at the gym.

This was where God began to turn everything around although, of course, it wasn't where it all started.

1

IN THE BEGINNING
THERE WAS PINECREEK

THE SUN WAS HOT THAT DAY WITH AN EVER-SO-SLIGHT BREEZE. THIS SUMMER DAY DID not hide any of the beautiful colours it helped to create. Tall green spruce trees and thick lush grass were accompanied by beds of beautiful flowers planted by our mothers. Swinging on tire swings as high as our legs would allow us were my usual sidekicks, my cousins Rachel, Loretta, Brenda and Janice. Our faces were warm in the sunshine and we were singing at the top of our lungs our new favourite song: "How far is heaven? I want to know. How far is heaven? I want to go."

We sang it over and over again, imagining the tender emotions of the little girl in the song whose daddy had passed away. When we tired of that song we soon began singing other favourites: *This Little Light of Mine* and *I Have Decided to Follow Jesus*. I'm sure all of Pinecreek had a front row seat at our outdoor concert as they went about their daily chores on the farm.

I was born in the Pinecreek Hutterite colony. The year was 1976 and Pinecreek Hutterite colony had been established just a few years before, in July 1972. My grandfather, Sam Maendel, had had a vision to start a Christian community and after he spoke with his brothers-in-law, they worked to accomplish this goal—and, with less than a dozen families, Pinecreek colony was founded ten miles north-east of Sidney, Manitoba. My grandfather and his wife Rachel had authentic faith and loved the Lord. My grandfather wanted freedom for his thirteen children and wanted to be free from a legalistic faith.

Let me tell you a bit about the Hutterites. Hutterites share common roots with Mennonites and Amish of Mennonite descent, tracing their origin back to the sixteenth-century Anabaptist movement that called for adult baptism.

Hutterite history involves a succession of migrations in search of religious freedom. Hutterites moved from Germany and Austria to Hungary and farther south to Transylvania (today's Romania), then north to Kiev in Ukraine, south to the Molotschna in Ukraine near Alexandrovsk, Zaporozhie, then across the Atlantic to the Dakotas in the USA and finally during World War I up to the Canadian prairies.

There are three distinct Hutterite groups (Schmiedleut, Dariusleut, Lehrerleut) each named after their founder. The group I belonged to was founded by Michael Waldner who, as a blacksmith, was called Schmied-michel (the German word for smith is schmied) and thus our group is known as Schmiedleut. (The Dariusleut was named after its leader Darius Walter, while the third group that left Russia was led by Jacob Wipf, a teacher. Since the German word for teacher is Lehrer, his group was called the Lehrerleut.) The Schmiedleut Hutterites founded six colonies near Elie, Manitoba; these have grown to number over 100 colonies, with between 50-120 people typically living in a Hutterite colony. My mother and my father's mother both came from the first Schmiedleut colony; Michael Waldner was a distant relative of ours.

The Hutterite religion is unique in that they believe in community of goods, in which all material goods are held in common, a way of living out Jesus' commandment to love neighbour as self. Most colonies are sustained through farming as a livelihood. Church services are held daily in most communities, forming the core of Hutterite devotional life. Hutterites have always practiced both a modest and simple uniform dress code, originally based on the German and Austrian national costume. Men in the Schmiedleut group in Manitoba wear many types of mostly dark-coloured casual jackets that are in most cases homemade. Women wear either a one piece to two-piece dress, according to preference. Women also wear a tiechel (head covering) which is mostly plain black. In some colonies woman wear a black apron on top of their dress to church, though most have eliminated this.

My parents, Elie and Susanna Maendel, named me Susan Jane Maendel but they decided on the way home from the hospital that they would call me Jenny. So there it began. My birth certificate, of course, didn't change.

Though I only lived in Pinecreek Hutterite Colony for eight years, those tender years moulded me into who I am today. My memories of Pinecreek are so full of fun, imagination and adventure. We were a close family and there was quite the group of cousins my age. My cousin Ian, being the oldest, taught me how to ride a bike and—if you call being tossed out of a water tube in the Pinecreek

River swimming lessons—my cousin Randy taught me how to swim. Ian and Randy were our oldest cousins and we thought they were the captains in our ship of fun. I had three brothers: Conrad, Glen, and Elias, with me being the eldest. Conrad was only eleven months younger than me, so he was quickly claimed as my playmate and was forced to comply with all my adventures. Whether it was tea parties, sandbox fun, or a simple stroll on the sidewalks adjoining the family homes around Pinecreek, he was close by my side. That is until my mom put an end to this happy little duo and informed Conrad that he should be hanging out with our little brother, Glen. Conrad and Glen were only a year apart. I wasn't fazed by this interception because my cousins Loretta and Brenda were not only my cousins but they were my ever-so-close sidekicks—we were as close as sisters and still are to this very day. Loretta and Brenda also had a younger brother named Jason who happened to be the same age as our Glen so they too quickly formed a trio. Glen and Jason were notorious for getting into a lot of mischief and always had the perfect lookout, Conrad. (He must not have been the best lookout because they usually got busted.)

My Uncle Lorenze was my dad's brother and Loretta, Brenda, and Jason's father, but he was also a fun-filled adventurer. When he saw us running through a mud puddle as fast as our rubber-boot-clad legs could go, he had an even better idea. He attached the riding lawn mower to the metal wagon which was used to haul laundry baskets to and from the laundry facilities on the colony. When he hollered for all of us to climb in, we ran as quickly as our excited little bodies could go. There were nearly a dozen of us kids cramped together. He started the engine and off we went as he called back, "Hang on!" Through the mud puddles we went, thrilled. All the while, our stunned mothers stood nearby, yelling for him to knock it off, but that just encouraged him more. The next time there was an opportunity for Uncle Lorenze to have his very own mud bog, he fastened a wooden playpen to the wagon—for our safety, of course. So off we went through the mud puddles. Uncle Lorenze baited our mothers by asking us, "Shall we go through the mud puddles again while your mothers watch?" To this we all eagerly responded, "Yes! Yes!"

It was not all fun and games. Young Hutterite girls have lots of responsibilities on a colony. I can recall so clearly before the age of eight scrubbing socks on one of those old-fashioned wash boards, assisting Mom with hanging clothes on the line, tidying the house, washing floors, babysitting younger siblings, and doing dish duty in the community kitchen. Young girls were usually stuck drying the dishes. I loved seeing how fast I could dry the cutlery, and we would usually make a competition out of it. On certain occasions, one of us would be chosen to help with the rinse sink. Oh, how we took that glorified spot as if just having received the highest promotion!

I loved to clean, probably because of the cleaners I got to use. Of course we used good old Mr. Clean but Hutterites also make their own soap and it's a fascinating process to watch. One day, when I was washing floors at home, my cousin Rachel came over and she soon joined in. During the mission, I discovered a product called Comet. Why had my mother never shown me this beautiful product? I soon convinced Rachel that we should go all out. We washed walls, floors, table, chairs, counters, and finally the entranceway stairs with this new product—everything smelled so fresh and clean. My mother was going to be so impressed, I thought. I readied my little ego for all the loving words she would surely bestow on us. We had gone out to play but we were close by when my mother returned from that day's gardening task. As she opened the door I heard her gasp. I was confused by her shock and quickly went to see. Now I was the one in shock as I gasped: our shiny, clean haven was now covered in white film and smears, the evidence of our little hand scrubs on all the surfaces. As I looked up at my mom's shocked gaze, I understood why she had never told me of this beautiful new product before.

One thing that has always been important to me is how something smells. I was sure that I had been put on this planet to ensure that everything has a pleasant smell, so with this personal mission I formed an expensive habit. My father would sometimes purchase an expensive bottle of perfume for my mother. I was always so fascinated by the beautiful bottles holding this precious liquid. They looked so elegant sitting there on my mother's dresser. So, to finish off the chores, I thought that the perfect touch would be to just spray the perfume pump once. Yes, just once, I would instruct myself. It didn't take long before I added the whole house to my mission. Just one spray per room would be perfect. Well, my zealous nature soon went way overboard. My mother recalls coming home from the community kitchen after helping roll fresh buns for all the families for the week, and being irritated as she smelled her expensive perfume soaring through the summer air. Apparently I emptied more than one bottle on my routine missions. I can remember her coming home on one of those occasions and how furious she was. I remember her tone was one that told me she had reached her limit. The next day when I came home from German school (a class that was both before and after school where kids learned to write and read the language), she informed me of a new installation in her bedroom. It was an invisible electrical wire that ran across the entrance of their bedroom. If I dared enter her room when she was not there, then I was sure to be met with a huge *zap*! (I discussed this memory with Mom awhile back; she remembered the empty perfume bottles all too well. It was then I admitted to her the hours I spent lying on my belly trying to see that electrical wire, my eagle eyes wide open, wondering whether it was really invisible, and not daring to open the door to investigate further.)

There were cornfields surrounding our colony and Grandpa didn't waste any time getting us all together to help him with his irrigation system, moving the pipes to the right location. We all agreed quickly to help Grandpa for we knew that we were often rewarded with a trip to JJs, a restaurant/gas station a few miles south of Pinecreek. We all usually had a few dollars to purchase treats and our grandfather would often treat us to a pop and a pizza pop. I often think back and chuckle to myself wondering what the poor salespeople thought when they saw Sam Maendel pull up in his big blue van and a dozen or so eager Hutterite kids come running out.

One day, as the sun was beginning to let go of its hottest rays and we were just finishing our chores with Grandpa, he announced loudly that all of us should go home and wash up, and we would go on one of those treasured JJ trips after supper.

I had a plan. My parents had a large jar for loose change on the shelf in their bedroom closet, and as I reached for it, I was delighted that it was more than half full. Carefully I dumped it on my parents' perfectly made bed, thinking to myself that I would only take the silver coins. So there went my little thieving hands sorting through all the coins. Soon my large old leather Mexican purse was full of all the necessary stolen treasure and the crime scene was cleaned perfectly as to leave no evidence.

After supper the call came that Grandpa was getting ready to leave for JJs. I can remember my cousins looking at me strangely as my purse strapped across my chest seemed to be so heavy that I struggled to walk a straight line. (I wonder now if sin must appear this way to our Lord Jesus Christ as he watches over us from above.) We all piled into the back of Grandpa's blue van and we were on our way. Soon we were all in the store picking up our prized treats. I picked up my treasured treats and dealt with the cashier. Grandpa, who was patrolling the store to see where one of us may have needed some guidance, noticed my loot. "Goodness child! Where did you get all that money?" he asked in German. I explained, "Grandpa, it's mine. I've been saving for a while." What a guilty thief

I must have seemed. Everyone was climbing back into the van for the journey home, each holding a can of pop and a small bag of chips or candies—and there I was with my large two-litre bottle of root beer and my box of ketchup chips. Boy, was I going to have a feast! Grandpa had asked me a few more times if I had taken some money from my parents, and I, unaware of how guilty I must have appeared, kept denying any illegal activity. Things soon changed as my grandfather chose to escort me home personally and there revealed to my parents the rest of the stolen silver loot still in my purse. I soon had to hand over my prized purchases.

Christmas was a joyous time of year! The Hutterite Christmas traditions are filled with family, gifts and lots of fellowship. Hutterites celebrate the Christmas season as a three-day celebration December 25-27, as well as commemorating the visit of the wise men to baby Jesus on Epiphany, January 6. The Hutterites practise a communal distribution of gifts called Nicholas, after St. Nicholas of Myrna, whose story provides the legend behind Santa Claus. There would also be extra church services with lots of opportunity to sing cherished German and English Christmas songs. We girls all got new dresses and new clothes sewn by our mothers. Our Christmas dresses were beautiful and we usually received two or three.

For a few years in Pinecreek, we celebrated by piling into our community dining hall, since Grandma and Grandpa's place was getting a little too crowded. There was such excitement as each family piled all their presents in the wagons to be pushed to the hall. The wonder of Christmas was in the air. I remember when my grandfather convinced our uncle Tim to dress up as Santa to surprise all of us kids. Wow, we thought, Grandpa really did know everyone, even Santa! (My grandfather always had a back-up Santa ready too!) For the children of Pinecreek, we needed no further proof to know we truly were the most precious in all the world—Santa was spending the evening with us in Pinecreek. Even our dads took their turn sitting on Santa's lap.

I was a determined little girl and often heard my parents and relatives commenting on my big mouth. There were no areas where I lacked courage. "Stubborn!" I can still hear my Grandpa say. I knew my grandpa loved me but all my relatives agreed they could all do without my disrespectful spirit. I would often stand up for those who had been wronged. I knew I held the title for the most stubborn girl, and heard my family tell my parents that they had better find a way to harness the reins and break this stubborn spirit or there would be no end to my trouble. I now know that when Jesus looked at me, He saw a determined little girl whom He created, one who would have courage and strength. Sometimes when there is a very strong-willed child you only have to imagine the persevering spirit they will have as an adult.

Waiting to start school was excruciating for my cousin Loretta and me. All of our playmates were already in the small schoolroom, attached to the community kitchen and dining hall. Our colony was smaller so our schoolroom served as both a schoolroom and a church. Bored out of our wits, we came up with what we thought was a wonderful idea. We first began by throwing the smallest of pebbles at the outside wall facing us. Everything went smoothly until one of us heard our pebbles hit the untargeted window. We both let out a squeal of fear and ran for cover. Our next plan was to gather up all the jackets and to carry them outside. Wouldn't they all be so confused when they came out for recess? This went on for a few days as we were constantly challenging each other, but it soon became mundane to see them coming out and looking for their lost coats. On our final day of trouble-making, there had been a fresh rainfall and everyone's boots soon joined their jackets in the puddles. We had no concerns that the teacher would definitely be ready for us come September

We had been counting down the days until school began and were involved in every detail of the preparation, as over-excited kids usually are. On one occasion, I noticed that my mother was holding my registration forms and my eyes fell on a birth certificate. I scanned over the document and when I came to the name section, I was shocked to discover that my real name was not Jenny as everyone had been calling me, but Susan Jane Maendel. *What?* I thought in confusion. My mother explained that yes, that was what the document said but that everyone just called me Jenny. I decided I liked the name Susan—it was different and it was, after all, my *real* name. When my mother couldn't disagree with my reasoning and demanding nature, she simply gave in, probably thinking that it would make no difference. We both did not realize it would make a difference in the years to come.

When the first day of school did finally arrive, our teacher greeted us warmly. We were very thankful and as we were taking our appointed seats, she began informing the whole class that there was no further need to check the front entrance multiple times a day just to see where Loretta and Jenny had placed everyone's jackets and boots, or to see what we would try next. Everyone erupted in roars of laughter. Wow, we were famous! And we had made it to school at last! I remember thinking that this day just couldn't get any better. What I heard next proved otherwise. The teacher began calling everyone's name and to this they were attentively answering, "Present." I gasped: we got presents? I leaned over to my playmate, Loretta, "Did you know we were getting presents?" My cousins Ian and Randy overheard and tried to explain but their words just confirmed something even greater to me: "This is something we just do every morning before school work begins." We got gifts *every* day? I couldn't contain my enthusiasm as I sat there taking it all in. Eventually, as I watched every name get called and heard everyone confirm that, yes, indeed they were present, reality began to sink in: it was simply roll call and everyone was just replying that they were in attendance. The teacher very quickly decided that she too would call me Jenny for no one called me Susan and that solved that issue.

2 LET YOUR LIGHT SHINE

OUR DUPLEX HOUSES WERE AS COZY AND CLEAN AS OUR MOTHERS COULD MAKE THEM.
We usually got to enjoy our family homes at our cherished three o'clock "lunch". This time was for Hutterites everywhere the greatest coffee break ever—a restful time with your spouse and kids enjoying coffee or tea (yes, Hutterite kids love tea) and some freshly homemade baking. We would also enjoy chocolate bars and candy sometimes but although we were poor, our grandfather always worked hard to make sure we had a good portion of the best fruit available.

On one occasion, I was enjoying my snacks with my brothers Conrad, Glen, and Elias. Mom and Dad were having their usual conversations. I loved my dad's low voice as he discussed with Mom the tasks and frustrations of the day. Mom, being of a quieter spirit, easily listened without interruption. I let my mind wander but when my eyes caught sight of the picture hanging in our dining room I paused on the words written on it:

> LET YOUR LIGHT SO SHINE BEFORE MEN,
> THAT THEY MAY SEE YOUR GOOD WORKS,
> AND GLORIFY YOUR FATHER WHICH IS IN HEAVEN.
> MATTHEW 5:16

This familiar frame had been there always but this time my attentive spirit wouldn't let go of it. The yellow rays of sunshine wrapped around what would become my first taste of Scripture memory. I practised the verse over and over, challenging myself with the correct wording. This Scripture has never left me and now I know that those words were written by Matthew, one of Jesus' chosen disciples. These were Jesus' words during what would become known as the Sermon on the Mount. The book of Matthew was basically a play-by-play of Jesus' ministry. I had no idea as such a young child that this Scripture was supposed to be part of my destiny.

But there was a powerful movement of faith blowing through the Pinecreek Hutterite Colony. My grandfather loved the Lord and he was hungry for worship. Mutual friends of Grandpa would soon connect him to someone who would lead our very own evangelical tent meetings. The speaker was Allan Woursh, or Al as we would call him. Al was a Winnipeg city police officer who had a passion for Jesus. Al was ministering in Winnipeg when he was invited by the native evangelical group to attend their tent meetings on reserves in Manitoba. One of the native evangelists introduced Al to my grandfather who invited Al to preach at our colony. All of Pinecreek and some surrounding neighbours were saturated in a message of hope, healing, and the power of the blood of Jesus Christ. I loved the enthusiastic and passionate way the message was spoken, and the unique and diverse experience of these native evangelical tent meetings. I remember my spirit just drinking it up and all of us little cousins sitting in awe. My mother said these meetings were filled with the salvation message with an anointing from above. She also stated that those times of fellowship were crucial in their survival since Pinecreek's early years were times of tremendous difficulty: God brought them a powerful sense of hope, and a fresh sense of freedom swept over our colony, squashing any seed of legalism that was threatening to sprout.

(In January 2015 I had the privilege of meeting Al again. He was retired and living in Saskatoon, but he still looked the same to me, and those same blue eyes still flashed with excitement when he talked about those cherished memories of Pinecreek. Many of his memories were about my grandfather and his sons, how they loved discussing faith in the Lord Jesus Christ, the truth in Scripture and the importance of unlegalistic faith. They welcomed him in Christian fellowship and all he had to teach. Al said when he looked for evidence of fruit in Pinecreek, he saw lots of growth, lots of fruit. This also was confirmed by my mother. She recalled many occasions after hearing Al's messages on the goodness and power of God's Word, their spirits soared when entering the garden for work the next day. Al chuckled as he told me of the many times he had jumped right into the daily tasks found in colony life—butchering, harvesting corn, and gathering eggs. He still stands amazed at the time they picked 1200 dozen corn. He remembered my grandfather's generosity and humility, and recalled my grandfather's prize apple trees. I told Al that before they closed the casket for the final time at my grandfather's funeral, my brother Conrad had placed an apple blossom in his folded hands.)

The early years of the Pinecreek colony were hard.

Mom recalls so vividly how brutal hard labour was part of their normal day but that they tried to work together to make the best of it. All of us cousins can remember the great stresses that were evident among the adults. I guess that's what makes my fun-filled memories so miraculous.My best memories have to do with our famous movie nights where Grandpa and Uncle Lorenze would borrow films from the local library and show them on a film projector in our community dining hall. These were treasured times for all the families in the colony.

The German language is a strong language with deep vocals. Most people would even describe it as too rough-sounding. I loved it, however, and felt it to be powerful especially when it was spoken in anger. As a young child, I began to make the connection that anger and volatility were a way to gain power. I loved the energy it brought. In our home, anger was just a part of the norm and Dad had a definite volatile nature. Also, all of us kids were no strangers to discontent for our fathers who were brothers did not easily get along.

My mother was a quiet, shy, introverted woman when she first moved to Pinecreek on her wedding day, June 29, 1975. Moving to Pinecreek was definitely out of Mom's comfort zone, as it was for most brides who moved to their husband's colonies. (The Hutterite custom is that all females move to their husband's home colony.) No two Hutterite colonies are alike and they can be quite diverse. Sometimes I'm sure it feels like you are moving to a new planet. All of us can agree that it is an adjustment becoming acquainted with our significant other's family—how much more it would be to get used to a whole new colony! Thankfully, my mother had her sister Clara with her and soon her little sister Sara who would also marry one of Dad's brothers, my sweet Uncle Steve.

In order to survive, Mom became an artist at keeping all her emotions in, something my father didn't ever do. My mother became a champion at giving the silent treatment. (If you haven't already guessed it I definitely do not take after my mother!) As a child, I hated this silent treatment because I could never understand it. To keep quiet was next to impossible for me. I so longed for my mother's gift of silence in my growing years. I now understand, though, that in order for God to use me for my destiny, for His specific purpose for me, I must be vocal, courageous and bold.

As things became more difficult in Pinecreek and in our home, volatility increased. I began to see my mother begin to crack; there was a different tension in the air. One day, she cried, screamed and pounded her fists on the walls as we all settled at home after breakfast. I couldn't believe it: my mother had broken open. This was so unlike her, and my father soon took notice and became solemn. There was a shift that day like they had reversed roles somehow. In her outburst, my mother had made it known that things had to change in the way my father and his brothers had been acting. It left an eerie quietness in the air for the remainder of the day.

Later that evening, when my brothers and I were all in bed, there was a knock at the door. It was not the time you would be expecting company. I remember creeping out into the living room area where I saw my mother in the living room being consoled by my two aunts, while their husbands—my dad and his brothers—were talking by the front entrance. After some short comments, it seemed to get a little tense and then there were words of forgiveness, and voices began to crack. I remember holding my breath at what I was witnessing. All alone I stood, half-hidden by the dining room wall, so thankful that I was not in bed. My uncles walked up the steps and each embraced my father. They stood, all holding each other tight, with sobs and words of reconciliation, love and forgiveness. There was nothing but peace and humility in the air. I felt the love these brothers had for each other deep within. They united once again to try to endure the difficulties of that time, and to somehow make a way to figure out the great trials in their lives. I have never forgotten this memory and see it as a divine appointment since I was the only one that awoke and was witness to it. I remember how the tears stung the corner of my little eyes as I drank up every emotion that was exhibited in that moment. Our fathers and uncles were giants to all of us kids. As I witnessed this repentant spirit, I decided when I became an adult that there would be nothing that I couldn't repent of or forgive.

LETTERS TO HEAVEN

IT WAS THANKSGIVING WEEKEND AND I WAS EIGHT YEARS OLD. ON SATURDAY EVENING, my dad took our whole family to JJs for treats, which we enjoyed together while Mom and Dad drank tea and sang their cherished German hymns together. This would be the last time we would be together as a whole family.

Sunday morning was the usual: breakfast, followed by a morning church service. There was extra excitement in the air as we were anticipating a visit from our Grandma Anna, my mom's mother. My grandmother lived in Woodlands Colony near Poplar Point, Manitoba, but was visiting at a nearby colony for the weekend and was stopping in at Pinecreek on her way home. We were all so looking forward to see her and that was definitely the cause of the extra excitement in the air. Grandma Anna was a gentle soul and I loved her radiant face and her perfect complexion. She had the softest blue eyes you could ever imagine. I loved how she would break the occasional rule just to give you the gift of grace. We never left her house without a handful of treats and all of us girls would get to pick a necklace from the jewelry box in her closet.

It was a warm fall day, a slight breeze in the air warmed by the sun peeking through the clouds. My mother was enjoying an afternoon visit at my Aunt Clara's, and she and her sisters were waiting eagerly for Grandma to arrive. Brenda and I were in our house enjoying an afternoon snack of freshly sliced oranges. I remember we were all giggles as fresh orange juice sprayed through the air. My father had gone to finish some last-minute chores by the cattle barns and had taken my brother Glen with him to help. I'm sure he was trying to get through these chores quickly as he was also excited about the visit with my grandmother, for he loved his in-laws very much. (Mom said she had often been annoyed when she and Dad were courting because Dad and Grandpa would often be so busy yakking that she wondered if he had actually come to visit her or her father. Her father was a gentle, loving man who died when I was young.) At six years of age, Glen loved any opportunity to be a farm boy and especially anything to do with of course a tractor. He was all adventure and his nickname was Johnny Boy.

As Brenda and I were wiping up the kitchen counter after our snack, I heard a sound I will never forget. At first I thought it was the wind for it was a low howl, but then I knew it was not because as it continued it was interrupted with high-pitched screams. We quickly summed up the commotion as being the excitement of Grandma arriving and we raced to the window in our living room that faced the front yard. But what my little eyes saw out of the window caused me great confusion and, as the screams were now very loud, I felt my tummy do a large flip and then I sort of just froze. Brenda and I just stared in stunned silence. We soon realized that these were definitely not joyous, excited screams—they sounded horrible. My mom was covering her face with her homemade pretty white handkerchief in both hands, screaming uncontrollable sobs into it. Walking beside my mother was one of my aunts, holding my mother up, while behind my mother were the other women from the colony who also were crying with short groans and breaths. My cousin Brenda and I looked at each other, fear clearly covering our faces. Neither of us had ever been witness to such a confusing display of emotions. My tummy was still doing somersaults and my palms felt sweaty from the anxiety that was quickly taking over my whole being. When my mother uncovered her face momentarily for gasps of air, I could see her face was completely covered in both a state of horror and hopelessness.

The front door opened and now it was my mother and father holding each other. I remember my dad's crippling stance as he both struggled to walk and hold my mother up as well. He fell on the second step, and his arm still clung to my mother's shoulders. He reluctantly let go as to have enough strength to get up on two feet again. They managed to make it up the short three steps and I noticed blood smeared all over the side of my dad's face, his arms and the whole front of his dark green t-shirt. They made their way to their bedroom and I followed, standing in the corner of the hallway by the bathroom, hanging onto the corner of the wall, where I had a perfect view to their bedroom. Once in their room, Dad collapsed onto the bed. Blood now covered my parents' perfect white bedspread. My father, too, was crying and was inconsolable. What was going on? We knew it had to be something as horrible as death, but whose? No one ever told us the truth. We picked up the fragments that formed the horrible truth. *My little brother Glen was dead.*

I can remember the little voice inside my head: "You're the oldest. It's time to grow up, no more fooling around, no more silliness," as if I was giving myself a reality check that life was now never going to be the same again. I would be strong for my Mom and Dad. In that moment the little girl inside me more or less died, too.

Dad had been hauling a load in his John Deere tractor on rough terrain with Glen standing snuggly beside Dad's tractor seat. When Dad looked back to check on the load, my little brother must have slipped off; Dad did not realize until he turned around and noticed Glen was not there. Then, when Dad turned his head to look back, in horror, he saw Glen lying in the tractor tire tracks: he had just run over his six-year-old son. He ran, picked up my brother's crumpled body and then carried him two hundred yards. My Grandpa Sam and Grandma Rachel rushed Glen to the hospital in hopes that there was a heartbeat, with Uncle Steve and Aunt Sara driving Mom and Dad quickly behind. When they met the ambulance on the gravel road not far from Pinecreek, it was confirmed that there was no hope of Glen's survival, and Mom and Dad had turned around instead of continuing on to where the ambulance stood. They then had no choice but to face the reality that Glen was gone.

My parents were in a state of shock. Mom was surrounded by her family, and it was awful that our grandmother had driven into Pinecreek in the first moment after the accident, with a horrible feeling as she saw the ambulance and hoping her fears were not true, but it was also awesome that she could be there. Mom still tried to be strong but could not keep this all bottled up inside.

I will never forget the sight of my dad, my strong dad, now broken as he lay on the bed in a hopeless heap. Accident or not, Dad's grief would be much greater than any one of us could ever imagine.

No one could comfort the depth of his despair, which would take long to heal, years of highs and lows from anger to despair. It would take my mother many years to fully understand the damaged man that Dad was to become. The only way Dad knew how to deal with his pain was to build walls—emotional walls that, as Mom said, he began to construct the day my brother died.

The next few days were ones of confusion and attention of a kind that as young children we didn't know how to absorb. I was full of raw emotion as my brother Conrad and I huddled close. My younger brothers Glen and Conrad had been so close that many even thought they were twins. Conrad was just seven and our cousin Jason was six. Their precious trio was now broken. These two boys were lost in their grief and confusion. Our whole colony was shaken. How could it not be for a community that was so close? This was the first death in Pinecreek so a cemetery would now have to be made.

My uncle Lorenze made it his personal mission to keep Conrad and I right by his side. We spent much of our time in one of our uncles' arms whether it was Uncle Steve, Uncle Lorenze or my mom's brother, Uncle Andy. This was our little brother and they ensured that we had the best seat in the house. I will never forget their armour of love and protection. When things became too intense, Uncle Andy let us go to our rooms where we got some much-needed quiet time. I also remember the privacy of my room where I could see my dolls, play with my toys and try my best to be a kid again. All the while, Uncle Andy stood outside our rooms and periodically checked in on us.

It had been a cloudy day the day of Glen's funeral but the sun shone brightly when the casket was first brought into our living room for the funeral. It is Hutterite tradition that the casket is placed in the family home for the wake and overnight until the funeral. The day of the funeral, Mom was the first one up, as she later recalled, and was still in a sleepy haze when she walked into the living room. When her eyes fell on the precious casket, the reality hit her with such force that she almost fell down from shock. It was extremely difficult to have your family home turn into a place of mourning but I was glad Glen was there in his casket, as if he was somehow still a part of us, not gone yet. I was still a little girl, still hoping to hang on to any sense of harmony.

When it was time to close the casket and take it to the grave, our uncle Lorenze once again scooped Conrad and me into his arms, bringing us through the crowd to our parents and kneeling down so that we could say goodbye to our brother. This experience taught me to not fear death but to embrace it and to know that death is a real part of our destiny. The minister spoke words that confirmed that Glen was in heaven now, with the angels, and that Jesus was close to the hurting. I became so intrigued, so full of questions. I wanted to see where my brother was. I had so many questions I needed to ask him. Oh, how I wish now that I could hold that little girl, tell her to be patient, tell her little spirit that God had a plan and to trust Him always.

The next few weeks were a sad blur. My aunts and uncles were always nearby and my grandmother stayed for a few weeks. I was so glad my mother had her. What I can recall with such amazing clarity were my letters to heaven. My tiny fingers hurt from the hours spent in desperate writing. I wrote to God. I wrote to my brother, asking him what he was doing, what he saw, what it was like. I was so curious, so desperate for answers. I thought I only wrote a few letters but my mother says that I sometimes wrote ten a day, and that she regrets that she never kept them, although it is totally understandable why she wouldn't. Scripture clearly states, *"Come close to God, and he will come close to you"* (James 4:8, NLT). How amazing to know that when we reach out to God, he will meet us there. God would write me back years later at the perfect time.

There was a hole in our family after that. None of us spent time in the living room after Glen died. We were forbidden to talk about our brother in our home. My father refused to let anyone grieve. The only comfort came from our aunts and uncles. I was so thankful for the extra love we received. Our Uncle Lorenze and Aunt Clara were instrumental in every aspect of my life, and Uncle Steve and Aunt Sara were no different.

It is truly amazing to me how much our childhood plays a role in who we become as adults, but also how much damage can be done when we forget to cherish and take care of that precious child in each of us.

A NEW LIFE

THE STRESSES GOT MORE INTENSE AS MY FATHER'S RAW EMOTIONS LED TO MORE heated tensions between him and his brothers. Not knowing how to deal with my brother's tragic death, my father made the decision to pack up his family and move out of Pinecreek Colony.

I still remember the night our parents told Conrad and I that we were moving. We were so excited and mistook the adults' hustle around us to mean that this would be a new adventure for us. As Conrad and I watched and let our imaginations take over, there was no end to our dreams about what this new world could be for us. Just five months after my brother's funeral, we packed our belongings and moved to Portage La Prairie, Manitoba.

In our new residence, Conrad's and my newfound excitement was short-lived as the shock of the transition set in. The reality took its toll, and nauseating homesickness set in. I remember the pain of missing all I'd ever known, our dear playmates and extended family. I cried tears of pain to be back there again. Living on a colony meant being part of a bigger family, a church community. Shock and pain washed over Conrad and me as we looked around at our new surroundings. He took it harder than I did as change was something he never endured well; he even stopped speaking completely for a few weeks. We had not only lost our little brother, but now we had lost our dear friends who were as close as siblings.

My father had a sister who already lived in Portage with her husband and three children. Uncle Sam and Aunty Judy had never lived in the colony as a family but had both left when they were in their twenties. We had always loved going to Uncle Sam and Aunty Judy's, and their kids were close in age to my brothers and me. I really got along well with their daughters, Debbie and Samantha. Their family was supportive in our transition from colony life to the community of Portage, and Debbie really helped me with the shock of not knowing anyone my own age. Together we made many memories, and she was a valuable asset in my most difficult years.

My mother had to endure the most as my father's grief had become hardened. She moved about almost as if in slow motion, her crumpled heart having to also transition into a new culture while longing for her sweet boy who was no longer in her arms but now in the arms of Jesus. My mother did not leave against her will—she admitted later in life that she always had a longing to leave the culture she had grown up in—and she grabbed hold of this opportunity and was both brave and strong. She honoured and loved Dad, and cherished her wifely role. I have a very clear memory of the day I looked at my mother and father and vowed that I would not be as silent and honouring as she was. I would not honour a hardened man. (I would pay dearly for that vow but not as much as my poor future husband. I would repent of this later in life when I learned God's truth about marriage and his truth on godly submission.)

As if there weren't enough traumatic events in our lives, Conrad and I, two little ex-Hutterite kids, began public school in March of a school year. We didn't even get the luxury of being the new kids on the first day of school. Mom later recalled how her emotions of our first day of school took their toll on her, leaving her with a migraine for the day as she was so scared to send her two young children into the great unknown.

My school records and birth certificate still clearly stated my name as Susan Jane Maendel, and now gone were the days when I was Jenny in the classroom. I actually think it sort of helped to have a new identity with a new name to match, but I truly was Jenny and all my family and relatives still called me Jenny. Everyone who wasn't family called me Susan. It was just the way it was.

We were soon greeted warmly by all we encountered at Yellow Quill School. The teachers and students were so kind. I still cherish some of those friendships. Conrad, though, was picked on and teased from the very beginning. He was in grade two and the kids in the playground wasted no time telling him, "You look funny, you dress funny, and you sound funny...You're a Hutterite!" It was never far from our thought that we were different from these kids, and, although I wasn't treated as harshly as Conrad was, I have to admit that I was (and still am) very sensitive and aware of our differences. The Portage kids acted differently from my colony comrades who teased and played in a very different manner. I had had one advantage that was helpful in this transition: a non-Hutterite family had sent their children to the Pinecreek Hutterite School. We had differences from them but I was thankful that they had been part of our colony school experience.

The kids in my class were fascinated with my accent and the fact that I spoke differently. Some even thought that I couldn't count. Over and over they would ask me to count to three. I would count for them, "one...two...tree...." They would erupt with laughter. I was confused and wondered what was wrong with these strange children. This went on for quite a while until I heard one of them say, "She keeps saying tree instead of three." *That* was what they thought was funny? So I gave them a show and counted for them as much as they wanted. You should have seen them bust a gut when I got to "tirteen" or when I said "tirty-tree." Morons, I thought.

Everything was different. Their lunches were different, the manner in which they ate them, the way they acted. Looking back now, they were normal kids in an elementary school who were simply comfortable in their surroundings and confident for they had never faced big changes and never suffered a loss like the one that we had just suffered.

I can tell you that God is good and He was there with us. I can so clearly see the hand of God surrounding our family as I look back on this season. I especially loved my grade three teacher. Mrs Pallister was an older woman who could give you the sternest look but who also had a tender humorous side. Maybe she saved that just for me for she totally understood the adjustments that my family and I were making. She also knew my father. He had left the colony numerous times as a young man and had a lot of acquaintances in Portage. I don't know how she orchestrated this but I still stand astonished that a teacher would go to this extent to make a little girl feel so special.

She announced to our whole class that we would be studying letter-writing for our English lesson, and that as a twist we would actually be writing letters to a different culture. I remember the warmth that filled my heart when she surprised us all. "We will be joining Pinecreek Hutterite Colony in a letter exchange and I will be handing you each a student's name and information about them," she said as she walked up and down the rows of our class. "When you get your penpal's information, you can write back to them with some information about yourself." I loved Mrs Pallister for I firmly believe she saw my authentic spirit and did whatever she could to nurture it. Tears stung the corner of my eyes and a huge lump formed in my throat as I watched all my classmates. No one was as blessed as I was at what they were about to experience. Now they were calling out the names that had been handed to them, their new penpals. I sat there with a smile so huge it hurt as I heard my new classmates chatter, "I have Rachel", "I have Brenda", "I have Loretta", "I have Ian", "I have Randy". For the remainder of the short school year, I had a gift of little brief moments of my former culture—what a gift, what a blessing. Every good and perfect gift comes from above, just like Scripture says (James 1:17). Thank God for the teachers who are so authentic in their ability to reach those moments that change the lives of their students forever My life was changed by the many teachers I have had throughout my school years, and I thank God for them.

Between grades six to eleven, I had some bad experiences of the new culture and life that left scars. Well into my thirties, every time I was in a setting where the word "Hutterite" was spoken, chills would run up my spine. The damage was great, the comments cruel. It took years of sadness to finally overcome the reality of what had been stolen from both Conrad and me. Our culture had been so safe, so precious. We had been proud to be Hutterites and still loved our families greatly even now that we were ex-Hutterites. Our identity gradually shifted to the new culture and with that came a lot of ignorance. We faced people who lacked true understanding of our culture, the Hutterite people. That is the biggest reason that I chose to put so much history in this writing project—so that you would be able to enjoy a true picture of the beautiful Hutterite culture.

My parents faced many challenges with our move, too, one of them being that our new home was not ready for us as promised. This left us in limbo and we stayed with friends until we could move into our home. Our sweet family pet, our border collie Rex, had to stay behind until we were settled. This was sad for us and we couldn't wait to have him with us. Our family did grow closer while under pressure and we did pull together to make it through the tough first few months. Once again I watched my mom honour my vulnerable dad. It didn't take my parents long to find a strong church family. God had placed people in our paths during the tragedy of my brother's death and his funeral, and now we were quickly invited to their Christian assembly in Portage where astonishingly enough the pastor's wife, Donna, had heard of my brother's tragedy and had been praying for our family six months before we ever walked into her church. We formed a close friendship with the pastor and his family. Another godly confirmation was one my mother felt: while doing her weekly cleaning chores in our family home in Pinecreek, she had made a habit of listening to a devotion time on the local radio station. It was led by the same minister we now listened to every Sunday morning. It's so amazing to me how God continuously paves the path and lights the way. I recently spoke with this minister, Pastor John Drisner, who remembers our family joining their fellowship like it was yesterday.

The church was a Pentecostal church. The worship was passionate, you saw authentic faith everywhere and the large congregation was very loving. The love of God was preached and we had many friends. Dad found employment just northeast of Portage as a mechanic, and with this new job came with the opportunity for us to live right on the homestead of the farm where Dad was employed. When the house was ready for us to move in, we settled in and made it our home quickly. I have memories of Conrad and me working hard right alongside our mother to help this house look like home. Our new house was definitely a fixer-upper: it was a two-storey bungalow with the brown and white trim paint peeling off the outside of the house. There was an issue with the heat so before winter the woodstove would have to be replaced. Burning wood for heat was very new to us and I loved it as it made the house even cozier. Upstairs Mom decorated the kids' room perfectly with Smurf wallpaper—Conrad and I remember lying on our beds or on the floor and looking at all those cherished Smurfs.

Our yard was totally surrounded by large lush spruce trees which reminded me of the tall trees that surrounded Pinecreek. There was also a perfect climbing tree right beside the house. That elm tree was where we spent many summer days, just sitting up in the big branches, as it was perfectly fashioned for a quiet hideaway.

But, oh, how I wondered what my playmates were up to. They would so enjoy the new summer songs I was making up and singing. It was amazing how quickly new lyrics filled my brain. I definitely had no secrets for if the kitchen window was open my mother now knew every thought, emotion, or guilty thing I had done—all sung at the top of my lungs!

Conrad was up to his own adventures with our brother Elias following him around. Elias, now four years old, chummed with us more often. Elias was adorable: he had a slim build and the kindest eyes that allowed him to get away with anything. He was a spirited little man and he kept up with his older siblings well. His nickname was Ferlie, a nickname that came from the landlord on the sitcom *Three's Company*. The television Ferlie was tall and slim with big eyes and curly hair just like our Elias and the nickname fit since the resemblance was hilarious.

Unfortunately Conrad's summer adventures usually included arson and bomb-making, his newfound hobby. He was clever, but not smart enough to avoid the harsh whooping he received from Mom and Dad for almost burning down the garage. The bomb he used left little Ferlie covered in soot, with a little smoke coming from his curly hair. That was the final straw and my brother lost his cherished camping outing that was scheduled for the next weekend. Conrad was devastated but the punishment was great enough to end my brother's career as bomb and fire specialist.

On another sunny summer day, we were all out in the yard when my grandfather Sam pulled up to see how we were settling. We did not realize that he had a prized passenger who also was very eager to see us: our Rex! He ran into our arms and we were all a big bundle of love. We all took our turns loving him up and he was happy to receive all of it. Then we sat back and watched as Rex made time for his favourite member of our family, my dad. Dad loved his Rex and was well known for his purebred Collie pups as he sold many. Dad got down on one knee and eagerly showered his pet with words of love. Rex was one ball of excited joy. It's as if he was saying, "I can't believe I'm finally with you. Where did you all go? I'm so glad you sent for me!" It was definitely an awesome day.

HOPE IN THE COLOUR
OF PINK

AS THE SUMMER HOLIDAYS CAME TO AN END, THERE SEEMED TO BE MORE EXCITEMENT in the air than just the anticipated new school year approaching. This proved correct when our parents informed us that Mom had to go to the hospital soon because she was having another baby and that we would be staying with our neighbours who were also friends from church. We loved these friends for they had a cozy house and the best toys so our excitement soon built for this special sleepover.

Having another sibling also seemed awesome for a family who had lost a child, and the wonder of this new addition was something I thought about often. I remember that on any bad day, I would cheer myself up by thinking that maybe I was going to have a sister. If only Mom could guarantee that this could come true. *There had to be a way*, I thought, in my nine-year-old desperation. I had to come up with a plan. *Aha! I had it*! I would simply threaten my mother. It seemed harsh but I was very desperate for a little sister. I would wait until she was on her way to the hospital. When the time came, as I kissed her good-bye, I assertively informed my mother that if I wasn't going to get a little sister then I was simply just going to have to run away! I made sure she knew I meant every word of my threat. We would just have to see how my plan was going to work out for I was definitely deserving of a sister. My brothers I loved, but they were constantly breaking my prized girl toys and had no respect for my things. I so needed a girl in my court and obviously didn't think that the nine-year age difference would be an issue

Off we went for our sleepover. There was a lot of excitement in the air and our neighbours welcomed us warmly and we settled into play mode quickly. Later on, when the phone rang, I was called to the phone and was told my mother wanted to speak to me. My heart quickened as I grabbed the receiver and held it firmly to my ear. "Well," my mother said. "Are you ready to move out?" My heart skipped a beat. I was speechless. My plan had failed horribly—only a moron would make such a threat! But my mother quickly interrupted my thoughts. "You don't have to pack your bags because you got your little sister." I let out a shout, "*Really*? You mean I finally have a little sister?" Mom informed me that we now had a little girl, her name was Annemarie and she was big and strong. We would meet her soon. I handed the phone back and eagerly confirmed the news to my brothers who had already been told of our new pink arrival. Falling asleep that night, I was the richest girl in the world, and the luckiest, for thank goodness I didn't have to move out!

It is a Hutterite custom that, when a woman has a baby, her mother or one of her sisters will join her for one to two weeks to make sure she has the appropriate rest and support. This is called Obvoten, and it was my sweet Aunty Sara who was given permission by my Uncle Sammy (who was the boss at this time and who made decisions together with my grandfather) to still be allowed this cultural tradition. What a perfect picture of brotherly love. For even though we had left the Hutterite church, we were still family and in Pinecreek, blood was always thicker than any legalistic religion that one might think they have to bow to. I will always have honour for my father's brothers and for my Grandpa Sam who fought for this Christian foundation. When Auntie Sara arrived for her few weeks' stay, we felt we were royalty, for this was the type of aunt she was. She knew how to make you feel special and loved, and she had and still does have the biggest giving heart. Aunty Sara wanted children dearly but she and Uncle Steve were waiting on God's perfect plan for their lives. (After ten years, we rejoiced with them when God blessed them with two children of their own.) At this point, however, with no kids yet, every one of her nieces and nephews were showered with her amazing love and she taught me a lot about how to bless people with love (and treats). I was happy for my mom that she had her sister; Mom seemed to relax even more because of Aunty Sara's presence. I realize now that my mother had left the Hutterite colony while expecting her fifth child. I cannot imagine the added stress this must have been for a couple in an already overwhelmed world.

With our sister's arrival we were well into the new school year. Her arrival was even more special for we had something to share with all of our classmates— whether they wanted to hear or not, we were very enthusiastic about our new family member. This school year was definitely easier for we quickly fell into the routine and had some friendships secured. It was so nice to see my friends again and I bragged all about my little sister.

Anna was such a picture of hope for a broken family. My father's heart opened up again and he adored her. I longed for that same affection but my father was far too busy for annoying little Jenny. I had a determined spirit and a big mouth which likely didn't help. Throughout my childhood and growing years my father and I clashed. I took everything personally and was very intuitive to all the stresses my parents faced. I just so badly wanted to help, to make them feel better. Instead I was misunderstood the majority of the time, but I kept trying to gain my parents' love and acceptance. I have many memories of listening to any adults in conversation with my parents, just hoping to catch a dewdrop of something positive. If it happened I would take the words of affirmation and float with them back to my room, rehearsing the memory of that verbal love over and over.

The seasons were quickly changing from fall into winter, and there was extra work to be done to prepare for the cold Manitoba winters. Bringing in the chopped wood was something I enjoyed doing. It made me feel good knowing that I was helping to alleviate some stress from my parents. My father was a hard worker and had the strong work ethic that we as a family prided ourselves on. My father's temperament was always fluctuating so we knew when to help out and when to leave him alone. Once the wood was chopped, we did our part.

Then came Thanksgiving weekend and all the memories hit my family. It had been one year since my brother had passed away. We felt the memories so strongly that it felt as real as it had the previous year. My parents fell apart in the quietness of the evenings when it was just the two of them. The Christmas season was even harder. My mother recalled later that it was alcohol that took the edge off of my father's horrible memories in the days leading up to Christmas. My precious Dad. I wish I could have wrapped my arms around him for we all watched his pain as the walls went up again and in the pain he sheltered his heart. Only the birth of my little sister shed a new light of hope in those dark days. I'm sure it would have been harder had her sweet presence not been with us. Also this was to be our first Christmas away from Pinecreek and the beautiful traditions that Hutterites cherish. It would be difficult and we could see the dark cloud surround my father as the memory surrounded him once again.

The year before, my father had ordered a large John Deere tractor toy for both Conrad and Glen for Christmas before Glen died. A few weeks after my brother's death, one of the sales people told Dad that the tractors he had ordered were in and that he could pick them up at the parts counter. Dad came home in a crumpled heap. Glen's tractor still stood in their closet in our new residence, a fresh reminder of the toy Glen never got to open on Christmas Day.

We all did our best, and our new friends and church family were kind but could never understand our broken pain. Nobody other than our Father in heaven fully understood our need; this was proven to me by my greatest Christmas memory ever.

It was after supper not long before Christmas and we were in the living room playing while Mom and Dad were enjoying a hot beverage after the evening meal. There was a loud knock at the door and my dad answered it to find a few nicely dressed neighbours from our surrounding area. They were welcomed in and my father began a conversation. He knew a lot of people as he loved meeting new friends. We wondered what had brought these visitors to our home on a cold winter night. The answer came quickly as one of them announced that the community had heard of our family and the tragic circumstances that we had faced just the year before. They had decided a blessing was in order, and my father was handed an envelope and then the group began to unload the truck that had been backed up to our front steps. One by one, boxes were brought in.

Soon our entire kitchen was full of box upon box of Christmas goodness. There was a new Christmas sweater for all of us kids and even some presents to open for Christmas. The boxes included everything needed for a successful Christmas. The group was humble and kind and proclaimed they were simply a group of neighbours not affiliated with a particular church but representing brotherly love.

After our parents thanked them, they left us to enjoy our blessings. We knew in our hearts that the Lord's hand was upon this, as we all stood in awe and wonder at what had just been brought to us. This moment shifted our dismal outlook on the holiday to come and we felt the spirit of Christmas flood our home. My siblings and I held our presents and only imagined what was inside— just the simple pleasure of holding the wrapped gifts was enough. My parents later revealed that the envelope handed to my father contained five hundred dollars, a sum of money that they desperately needed.

I sat in my room and held my beautiful sweater. Then I hung it in my closet and sat admiring it some more. I held my new sweater as I lay falling asleep that night; it was so soft and I had never seen something so beautiful or elegant before. To me it was even too beautiful to wear but I would enjoy it for Christmas as it would go beautifully with the satin white and dark pink dress that my mother had made me for Christmas. I felt like a princess in my new Christmas dress, and God had given me a beautiful elegant sweater to prove He thought I was a princess too!

Our cousins also came to visit. There were winter days when we played for hours on the large snow hills made by our father and the snow forts proved we did not need to go into the house for a warm-up. Our fortresses had all we needed with even built-in sofas. It felt so good to be back together again with Loretta, Brenda and Jason. Conrad and I were on top of the world. They loved hearing all about our new life and we couldn't wait to hear all there was to tell about what sort of things we had missed out on at Pinecreek.

PORTAGE LIFE

WE WERE INVOLVED IN SOME KIDS CLUBS AND CHURCH WHICH TAUGHT US ABOUT GOD. I knew I loved the Lord and trusted Him but I started to form my own judgments along the way. These self-regulated rules would all but destroy the bridge from me to God. I started to believe that I had to have a gift or talent to be used by God and that if this was not evident then I was nothing. This void in my life grew bigger and bigger. I tried to believe in the truth that God did indeed have a plan for my life but it was difficult for me to be patient.

I had always had a temper on me but no one other than my immediate family ever got to see my temper tantrums. What then turned my guilt into condemnation? This cycle of belief that God disapproved of me and that I needed to shape up or He couldn't bless me. My self-esteem took a tumble as it does for many in the tough pre-teen and teen years. Being from a different culture was another twist in the web of identity confusion I often found myself in. *I should be like this person or that person. I wish I had that talent. I wish I looked like her.* One of my favourite hymns was *"Just as I am"*, but I let the lies of the condemning voice always distracted me. Was I Susan or Jenny? Did I want to live on a colony or not? Was it wrong to feel guilty for not wanting to live on a colony again?

God says to be still and know that He is God (Psalm 46:10). He also states in Jeremiah 29:11 that He has plans for us, plans to prosper and not to harm us. But I was impatient and stubborn, and, when you're not listening to the truth of God's Word, you very easily get lost in religion and forget that we are nothing without the help of a relationship with Jesus Christ.

I was lamenting all these thoughts once again during a drive home from church on Sunday afternoon; Dad had the radio station tuned into our local station which I loved. On this particular day, the most beautiful voices drifted through the radio and filled my heart with their amazing lyrics. I loved the words and felt they had been written just for me. The trio were Dolly Parton, Linda Ronstadt, and Emmylou Harris, and the song was *Wildflowers*. I decided then and there that this song would become my anthem:

WILDFLOWERS
The hills were alive, with wildflowers
And I was as wild, even wilder as they
For at least I could run, they just died in the sun
And I refused to just wither in place.
Just a wild mountain rose, needing freedom to grow
So I ran fearing not where I'd go
When a flower grows wild, it can always survive
Wild flowers don't care where they grow.
And the flowers I knew in the fields where I grew
Were content to be lost in the crowd
They were common and close, I had no room for growth
And I wanted so much to branch out.
I uprooted myself from home ground and left
Took my dreams and I took to the road.
When a flower grows wild it can always survive
Wild flowers don't care where they grow.
I grew up fast and wild and I never felt right
In a garden so different from me.

I just never belonged I just longed to be gone
So the garden, one day, set me free
I hitched a ride with the wind and since he was my friend
I just let him decide where we'd go
When a flower grows wild it can always survive
Wildflowers don't care where they grow.

Whenever I heard this song on the radio, I begged Dad to turn it up. This was and still is a favourite song for if I ever felt lost or misunderstood the words reminded me quickly of who I was and the courage I had within.

My parents were finally able to purchase our first home when I was thirteen, near Edwin, Manitoba. I still struggled with my ups and downs and the confusion I had with religion. There were godly mentors and youth pastors in our congregation, not to mention a strong core of kids our age. There was never a time growing up where my parents did not surround themselves with a strong faith base. Friends told us about a family Bible camp in eastern Saskatchewan near the town of Weyburn. Trossachs Bible Camp was a Pentecostal camp and we spent five or six summers taking the trip to camp and I loved it. Camp reminded me of living on a colony. I remember our family being the happiest in those times and I am so thankful for those memories.

But raw emotions were still the norm at home. My parents argued a lot about finances and family priorities but we tried to keep this volatility secret as we would be very embarrassed if anyone was to witness this anger. We had a lot of family friends and enjoyed the company and friendships with families from our church. I guess one imagines that these stresses occur only in their individual homes but now I know that all families are different and no family is perfect.

My father and I clashed most of the time and often Dad gave the impression that he completely loathed me. There was a time where I couldn't even walk across the living room to the kitchen without him verbally abusing me. I felt like I could do nothing right. It always seemed he was stressed to the max, and one look at me sent him over the edge.

There was one time, however, that made me thankful my father had ignored me a little. My friend Ramona had introduced me to a new product called Sun-In™, which promised to turn our hair blonde. Just before my dad picked me up from Ramona's house, I drenched my dark brown hair with Sun-In. Dad didn't feel like talking and easily ignored me most of the way home. I was caught up in a daydream when he snapped me back to reality. Just before we reached home, he suddenly looked at me and said, in German, "Dear God, child. What on earth have you done to your hair?" I quickly looked in the side mirror and gasped. My hair had changed colours completely from dark brown to platinum blonde during the ride home: he couldn't ignore that!

Both my parents worked full time. Dad also found it hard to say no to people asking for help, since he was a mechanic and fairly good welder. Dad had a lot of ups and downs with jobs. Mom tried her best to remain supportive and also protective in our home but Dad's ups and downs were exhausting. Mom would work hard and did her best to smooth things over but you could see the weariness in her eyes and sometimes she struggled with empathy. She would simply expect Dad to snap out of it, and in turn I watched my mother tear down a broken man even more with her silent treatments and looks of disapproval.

At school that year, for the first time I was involved in an extracurricular running club after school. I had long forgotten my days of running races on Pinecreek Colony as a little girl and I loved the feel of the endurance of the final sprint. I also loved the hurdles and I excelled in them. In my track meet I set new records in both short distance and long distance races and the hurdles. I can recall my mother sitting at the sidelines cheering me on and then looking in amazement at the powerhouse I became on the final lap. Mom told me later that people stopped her and commented on my speed, wondering what she had been feeding me. I finally felt I somewhat had a gift!

Dad soon found me a part-time job working at Robin's Donuts. I would work after school and on weekends and my parents graciously drove me back and forth. I loved this job and it still stands as my favourite place I ever worked. I learned a lot of things from my four years there. My boss, Bernie Wright, his wife Vivian and their three children taught me so much about working with the public and mentored me in this job. My people skills improved both my work ethic and my sense of pride. I was a natural hard worker and loved being employed. I loved that my dad had believed in me and he was proud that I proved him correct. I loved seeing Dad at the coffee shop interact with all the customers as he waited for my shift to end.

Sometimes my father found extra employment on weekends and would allow Conrad and me to join him. We worked with Dad at the chicken farm just south of town and he let us come along so we could earn some spending cash. I was very brave until we got to the part where we had to go into the barn in the dark and catch the chickens and load them into crates and then into a waiting semi trailer. I told my dad of my fear and he became rather tender-hearted, telling me some little tricks on how to avoid injury, to move past my fear and to try one chicken at a time. My dad stayed with me until I was brave enough and my courage grew .

Conrad and I also spent a few weeks every summer going back to Pinecreek. This was an incredible time and something that was usually unheard of but once again the legalistic religion was weighed against family blood ties, and our blood was thicker than religion. Looking back now I am so thankful that my uncles and grandfather allowed Conrad and me the opportunity to spend so much time there in summer. Life wasn't always easy and God knew that we still needed to be a part of this culture—for this I say thank you to my heavenly Father. Conrad and I would always make a contest of seeing who could see the cherished JJs sign first. During the summer holiday visits, we would transform back to Hutterite life and I would become Jenny again. I loved to be called Jenny for I felt I was more of a Jenny but decided that in the outside world I was better suited as Susan.

7
HE LOVES ME...
HE LOVES ME NOT

WHEN ONE IS BORN "BOY CRAZY", AS I WAS, ALL DAYDREAMING IS SURROUNDED WITH the crazy questions of wondering who would be the boy of my dreams. The thoughts drove me crazy! At seventeen, I cherished my relationship with God and believed that Jesus was the light in my path but I was desperate for love.

I still had my job at Robin's Donuts and my pocket change seemed to give me the financial freedom to want to rebel more than usual. I had been attracted to a different circle of friends and that summer seemed to be one of endless freedom. My parents put up a little resistance and I didn't like this—my friends had their freedom so why couldn't I? That's where lies began to work increasingly in my heart. My spirit was urging me to keep a steady path but my flesh was pulling in a different direction. I was busy with work, and Dad and I had declined to attend family camp due to work, but really my plans were to try to get more opportunity to hang out with my new crew.

One weekend, my father asked me to spend the next day with him and we would do some quality-time activities together. This was something I had longed for for so long but I now did not care anymore: I wanted to be with my friends and that was final. The whole weekend went horribly and it was one I will regret for as long as I live. My father intervened a couple of times, trying to deter me from my friends but I was not having it. I was both furious and embarrassed when my friends witnessed my dad force me to get in his truck and go home where I belonged. A few minutes later a car pulled up and I was shocked to see that my friends had followed us home and that they were now calling me to quickly jump in. Without a moment's hesitation I was in the car, and off I went. It didn't take long for me to feel sick to my stomach at what I had just done. It was a bittersweet night and I hurt inside at what my father must have thought when he came out and found me gone.

That summer of 1993 was one where I finally threw all my cares to the wind, and the morals that I had cherished for all my life were now gone. The lie that had been speaking into my being said that there was no point to God's rules, to the righteous path, that it was all stupid—look at all of my friends who were having more fun making their own rules. It definitely didn't help that one of my new friends was also from a very prominent Christian family in our church—it added more fuel to the sinful cause. These were not a rough group, or into any criminal activity but they definitely lived by a different moral code than I had ever thought I would follow.

By the end of summer I had done things I thought I never would—including a two-week runaway stint that led my parents to believe I could have been left for dead somewhere. When I finally went home and had done my best to repent to my parents, I knew the damage was great for my father was wounded and solemn. He had tried to protect me and I rejected him. In turn, I thought that what I had done was unforgivable and I began to wrap myself further in this new lie and so decided to walk away from my faith. I was done with Christianity!

In September I started dating a boy my father definitely didn't approve of. He was native and my father judged him unfairly. I cared for him deeply and my mother tried to be supportive but couldn't convince Dad, and the tensions reached a place they had never reached before and I had to move out. I dropped out of high school and decided to work full time. By July 1994, I was pregnant. I decided to abandon my relationship with the father of my child. I was ashamed and lost in disbelief that I could actually be a young teenaged mother. I never had imagined this for my future but in my cowardice, I wasn't about to admit to anyone that I had actually planned this pregnancy in an attempt to get people to give my relationship with my boyfriend a chance. My parents didn't want to see my face and my father dealt with my situation by lamenting to all who would listen. Soon everyone knew of my situation and thought I was an evil human being for causing such stress to my parents.

Scared and young, I ran into the open arms of my Uncle Lorenze and Auntie Clara. My Aunt Clara and I were extremely close. She had been there to nurture me through all my life and I still cherish her for all she did for me. My father's two sisters, my Aunt Helen and my other Aunt Sara, lived in Winnipeg and were also supportive of me at this time. I can also recall my grandfather wrapping his arms around me as I wept, and telling me not to be scared. He told me that I should come to the evening service and he would show me what our Heavenly Father would say to me right from the Bible. My grandfather preached a sermon on God's grace, telling me that I was God's child and that I was precious. He clarified very clearly that God loved me and this child; my weeks in Pinecreek were very loving and protective and I was taken in just as I was. I also spent some time with other family members who also treated me well and I was happy to have a few weeks with them.

Eventually my parents and I reconciled and I moved back home. My dad was very quiet and my mom tried to be very supportive as usual, making me maternity clothes. I stayed inside my shell of shame, spending a lot of time alone, my only friend being my pet cat. The baby's father could never find it in his heart to forgive me for abandoning him. He made it very clear that he cared nothing for me and it saddened me that I was not worth fighting for.

My father's gentle spirit came out when my mother and I found some baby furniture and we needed him to pick it up. Unloading the rocking chair, my father sat down and made his very own grandpa joke while Mom and I sat there drinking it all in. My father was indeed excited to be a grandfather.

A serene peace filled me over time and I knew I would be okay. I was also getting excited to meet this little bundle growing inside and wondered what my child would look like. I decided if the baby was a boy that I would name him after my favourite character on *Party of Five*, a new television show I enjoyed very much.

It was important to me that I remain responsible and independent so I secured an apartment for me and my unborn child. I still worked at Robin's Donuts and had earned enough hours to be eligible for maternity benefits for a year.

On March 24, 1995, I gave birth to my son and named him Bailey Aaron Maendel. He was beautiful, and motherly love wrapped around me when I first held him. My mother had not left my side during my labour—she was an award-winning birthing coach and I was so thankful she was there—and my father sat in the waiting room and held his very own prayer meeting. My father held my son and I heard him say with emotion in his voice, "He looks like Johnny Boy," and then my father's demeanour changed. In the days that followed, we soon realized my son's birth had been another trigger for my father. He had an emotional breakdown.

I will never forget when my doctor tapped me on the head gently as he gazed at my son, and said, "Very nicely done." I thought that to be the perfect compliment.

I had a lot of family stop in and I was showered with love and gifts but I still felt I was unworthy of God's grace. My family threw me a baby shower and so did my co-workers. Our church family was as supportive as they could be but my baby shower was not allowed to be in the church due to the fact that I was an unwed mother. This definitely was a reality check that I didn't fit the bill to be a redeemed daughter—I decided that religion and faith were not for me. I had taken a different path in life and it would take me years to get back to the life God wanted for me.

My cousin Loretta was granted permission by her father to come help me in the first few weeks after Bailey and I got home. I was so thankful that Pinecreek Colony was still very much a part of my life.

When Bailey was nine months old, his father and I found ourselves trying to reconcile to be a family. We had a few good months but it was not easy: we were so young and in many ways, he was never given a fair chance. Since my mother had been such a constant support in my life, her control was overwhelming, and once again Chris and I gave up. I remember the emotional goodbye and his words, "I just can't take how you get hurt because of my presence in your life." I am thankful that Chris gave me a beautiful son for I could not imagine life without Bailey. I promised myself that I would allow no future father figure to ever disrespect my son's biological father. He will always have a place in my heart.

***

In 1997, I sat very proudly with my son on my lap: I had achieved my dream of completing high school, going to school full time and waitressing part-time. There had been no room in my life to date anyone although there is one memory from that period that will always stay with me.

In my final months of high school, I was hanging out with my friend when I spotted the hottest guy I had seen in a while. He was a dream and I could instantly tell he was a farm boy and likely a cowboy because he wore his jeans and cowboy boots in a very confident manner. His eyes were light green and complemented his light brown hair well. I couldn't stop staring. I asked my friend who he was. My friend said, "Oh, that's Shaun Rumancik." I still couldn't help but think that he was perfectly my type of guy. Of course my friend got the message to him that I thought he was cute but his return reply was that he wasn't interested. I would see him around town after that and he was still as cute as ever.

Over the next few years, I was in a relationship with a man who was very protective and who cherished me, teaching me how it felt to really be loved. We wanted different things in life so eventually we separated but it was through him that I secured my job with McCain Foods and had the life I had longed for. Our work crew did many things together on our days off, like paintball games, barbecues and dancing at our favourite night club. My mother took my son to church with her but I was working shift work and made it very clear that I was not interested in church. I still talked to God and believed but did not pursue my faith any further. My parents enjoyed having Bailey, and my father had a special bond with my son. Mom and Dad seemed to be finally enjoying some good years: everything was falling into place and my father's career path was widening. My little sister was now ten years old and was becoming the perfect little babysitter and I reminisced back to my youth of being her age and helping out with childcare. Anna and I were nine years apart, and Anna and Bailey were also nine years apart.

My cousins at Pinecreek were still very much in my life, and Bailey and I still spent time in Pinecreek, although there had been a shift in Pinecreek that meant they were re-evaluating some of their religious structure and were tightening the reins on ex-Hutterites coming freely as before. My Uncle Lorenze and Auntie Clara were still very close to me and I remained respectful to the new Hutterite standards. My Aunt Sara's youngest, Steven, was only two years apart from Bailey and they formed a close bond.

My cousin Loretta called me one day and to my surprise asked me if I would be a part of her wedding celebrations. I was so honoured and asked her how this was possible. Unless you're living in a Hutterite colony, you are usually not permitted to attend a wedding let alone be a part of it. Having left the colony at such a young age I had never witnessed any Hutterite wedding ceremonies. She informed me rather quickly that she had asked her dad, and then my Uncle Lorenze had asked the board of Hutterite members if this could be allowed, and their reply was simply, "Yes, as long as she doesn't make any trouble." I still chuckle at their response as I have never thought of myself as a troublemaker.

A Hutterite wedding is a joyous affair and usually fills the better of two weekends. It is a time of happiness and celebration—a chance to see old friends or make new ones. Traditionally, the groom-to-be goes to the bride's colony with friends and family for what is known as Aufred Hulba a week or two prior to the wedding. On this Sunday afternoon or evening, there will be a gathering in the bride's home consisting of elders, friends, and relatives and youth where the groom-to-be publicly asks the parents' consent for their daughter's hand in marriage. There is a lot of well-wishing, admonishment, and advice from elders, friends and relatives; this is a festive time, followed by a fine supper. I was present at this event for my treasured cousin Loretta. It was one of the most inspirational occasions I have ever witnessed in the Hutterite culture.

We sat in the living room of my Uncle Lorenze and Aunt Clara's home, and the house filled with all the people who knew Loretta, the chairs lining the whole living room. On behalf of Loretta, they said many beautiful words and there was great honour in the room. I was both nervous and excited for Loretta: I knew how difficult it was for her to be in the centre of attention. It was such an awe-inspiring few hours. Anyone could only wish that those words would be spoken over them during an engagement celebration. Loretta's character was praised and it was made known that Pinecreek would be losing an incredible woman. Her father openly wept as he admonished his future son-in-law to make sure he realized the precious gift he had now earned. Since her dad would not walk her down the aisle (as this is not a part of the Hutterite tradition), this event could be seen as a beautiful verbal walk down the aisle.

Since the wedding takes place at the groom's colony, many of the bride's colony do not travel to the wedding so the Hulba is their only chance to celebrate with her. Young people sing far into the night.

A day of the following week is usually put aside for the couple to obtain legal documents and for the couple's families to spend time together, often followed by a barbecue or a restaurant meal for supper. This time may also be used to take wedding photos.

The Saturday before the wedding, the bride will say goodbye to friends staying behind, and the couple will be escorted in a train of vehicles carrying the wedding party to the groom's colony. The arrival of this motorcade is a merry event. An organized confusion of shouting, coloured balloons and honking horns lead the bride and grooms into the colony. The bride and groom are greeted and welcomed by members of the community. Shortly afterwards, there is a short church ceremony, and other activities similar to the previous Sunday celebration.

The wedding ceremony takes place Sunday morning where at the end of a lengthy sermon on Christian conduct on marriage, the couple stands before the assembled church, exchanges wedding vows and are pronounced man and wife. Following the ceremony a traditional midday wedding meal is served. Around three in the afternoon is yet another gathering, a continuation of the previous evening's activities and entertainment, with singing and maybe poetry or a power point presentation specifically created for this event. Snacks and desserts are served here as well.

When I returned from Loretta's wedding, I felt like I could not live in the reality of such a fairytale fantasy of finding love and then celebrating with such honour and Christian standards. I still had a lot of things I needed to figure out.

PRAYING FOR A DAD

BAILEY AND I SHARED A COZY BASEMENT SUITE AND WE BOTH ENJOYED IT JUST BEING the two of us. We read *Charlotte's Web* over and over before bed, enjoying giggles and snuggles, and enjoyed movie nights together. I tried to be fun and enjoy our little moments since I didn't get to see him very often due to my twelve-hour shifts. I felt stressed on many occasions so these memories are most precious to me. Being a single mother was something that I took very seriously and wanted to do my best. I had a huge fear that I would fail and lose control and have an unruly child so I kept the reins tight. I guess every parent has some of those fears when they are first-time parents but the anxiety is sometimes much worse for a single mother. It definitely was for me. I didn't want anyone condemning me as a mother. I regret being so strict and full of fear.

As Bailey neared the kindergarten stage, he was tender-hearted, reminding me a lot of his easygoing father. He was also starting to ask lots of questions about a daddy as he had seen fathers picking and dropping off their kids at daycare. He was extremely close with my father and brothers but it wasn't the same and we both knew it. Bailey's father and I had made an agreement that I would raise Bailey on my own. I wonder now if that was selfish, especially because it left a hole for a daddy in Bailey's life.

My father was concerned for me to find a good man so he had been encouraging me for the past few years to petition God for a noble man and to ask God to redeem my past choices. I just rolled my eyes when my father told me this for the first time, but he kept persisting and my mother was in on it too. So I thought that I would humour him one day. I called him in the morning and told him something was wrong. When he asked what it was, I told him I had asked

God to find me a man. My dad was really excited about this, but then I added the punchline, "When I woke up this morning, there was no man."

It had been a few years since we had laughed about this and I was starting to think that maybe my father was on to something, so the next time Bailey asked me that sobering question about a dad, I told him we were just going to have to pray for a dad. Bailey, who had enjoyed going to church with my mother, liked the idea and his brown eyes got really big with excitement. So that's what we did routinely during our nightly prayer times. When the months turned into a year, my little man turned impatient so I decided to tell him that when God looks for dads, He looks for the "best Dad ever".

But as evenings became the lonely parts of every day and sadness crept into my heart and took over, I found myself wondering, too, where this best dad was. My boy-craziness had definitely not subsided and I was always looking to the right and to the left for just the perfect man for me. On one of those lonely evenings, it came back to me about what Dad was often persistent to remind me of, to just pray for a man. I thought in the quietness in the night, "Okay, Dad, I will give it a try." This was my prayer: *Dear Lord, find me a man, a dad for Bailey.*

Tears stung my eyes as I began feeling unworthy. After all, I had walked away from my faith almost five years before and I was not committed to a church or a walk of faith so how could God hear me and answer me, the sinner, the condemned.

I chose to continue. *Lord, I want a country boy, a gentleman, someone who is kind, not jealous, and someone who is funny. A strong supportive man one who isn't insecure in his independence.* Wow! I thought, this is all coming out easily. So I continued. *I want him to be open to faith and oh, I hope he is cute. Please God,* I begged.

These were my desires and my petition in faith. I also knew that a man like this existed for I had met one when he and I were children. He was so cute and tall, with the most beautiful blue eyes. His dark hair made the combination almost too much and my knees felt weak around him. He had strong arms that proved he enjoyed his fair share of farm labour, a true country boy. After years of family visits, we found ourselves old enough to realize that our feelings for one another were more than a cute teenaged crush. I unfortunately was in one of the most confusing predicaments of my life, one that this boy was not aware of. But when the opportunity brought a moment when our lips could meet in a sweet first kiss, I decided to throw caution to the wind and pretend I was indeed from his world. For the weekend family visit, we held each other's hand, we kissed, we snuggled under the stars of the cool summer nights. Everything about our weekend was pure and he made it very clear that we could make it work, that we would somehow find a way for me to move to his world but I knew this could never be as we had left the Hutterite world behind. I knew this was a boy who would grow into a man of integrity and I so longed to share that future with him. Not only was this relationship never to be a possibility but I also had begun to believe that I could never be worthy of a man like this. What a horrible lie for a young woman to believe. I began to be ashamed for the predicament I had put him in. The pain of that time stayed with me for so long and made up a lot of the shameful ways I saw myself.

Now I was petitioning God for a man of character. Was I worthy? Was I forgiven? Was I heard by this high and mighty God that I most certainly had stopped following or serving? Somewhere in my desperation I still petitioned God for this man for me and my son. We still continued to pray for this best dad ever. After all we didn't have anything to lose. *Yes, Lord, a man of character. That is what I want.*

GIRLS NIGHT OUT

IT WAS NEARING THE YEAR 2000 AND LIFE WAS GOING WELL. I ENJOYED MY WORK. I
had lost forty pounds between my physically challenging job and working out at
the gym. I developed good friendships with people from work and I had a social
life I could only have dreamed of a few years before. Anna was in high school and
Mom and Dad could often be seen going for long walks down one of the country
roads by our house, holding hands in a secure love. We also enjoyed picnics in
our beautiful island park where Bailey would run free while his Auntie Anna was
in quick pursuit. Their age difference made them feel more like siblings than
aunt and nephew. Mom had started a new job a few years earlier and was more
secure with it. Dad had just purchased a newer truck and his custom baling was
also going very well.

The world was all abuzz about the new Millennium. I had been promised
tickets for the New Year's party of the year and was all excited and ready to go
out when at the last minute my friend informed me that the ticket had been
double-booked. My fun-filled plans had been cut short. I couldn't hide my
disappointment as I sat on the couch. Mom tried cheering me up by pouring
us a New Year's drink, and I tried to put on a smile for her but I was wondering
if this would be an insight into how the year 2000 would be for me. It began to
seem bleak as my bad attitude grew.

As February drew near, I began to feel my premonitions for this year were
going to be correct. There was also no sign of true love and I had all but given up
on my hope of ever finding that kind of love.

One day, my friend Jill called and said she had been noticing that I had been
down and out. She was in a crossroads in her love life and I enjoyed hearing her
vent about it. She proposed that two of us get all dressed up just for us and go for

cocktails. I really didn't have any desire and declined her offer. She pleaded and tried her best. She finally convinced me and I secured childcare for Bailey. Off we went all pretty and carefree! I felt confident in my curvy figure and had purchased some attractive clothing. My new haircut and highlights finished off my look. Jill and I sat in a booth and we quickly were into a fun-filled conversation. The music played as it softly filtered through the various speakers and it fit the rhythm and mood of our chats.

I noticed a group of about six guys had walked in and were securing their place around the pool table and surrounding area. They were laughing and seemed to be confident in their friendships. I recognized some of them and then continued to enjoy Jill's company. We didn't want to be interrupted as we were having a good time and our conversation was easily flowing. Then, as Jill went to get us more drinks, I took a second glance and noticed this one guy in particular. *Oh!* I thought, *it's him*, and I quickly reminisced back to where I had first seen Shaun Rumancik. When Jill returned to our table, I pointed this guy out to her and telling her my tale. The group continued to play pool and gave the two of us no notice. Jill and I finished our drinks and decided that the night was still young and we would check out our favourite night club.

We soon were on the dance floor and having a great time with all the friends who were out that night. It felt so good to dance and I loved more than anything to just move to the rhythm of the music and have no care in the world.

At some point, the group from the lounge arrived at the night club and began enjoying another game of pool. Jill and I finished up our set and took our seats which were ironically right next to the pool tables. We engaged in some conversation with the rest of our group who had been saving our table and had a few good laughs.

All of sudden my eyes locked with Shaun Rumancik's. I decided I needed another drink and thought I would take the long way around, walking right past the boys playing pool. "Oops," I said as my hips brushed against the pool cue that Shaun was holding, I apologized with a flirtatious tone and he rolled his eyes. On my way back, I noticed that he was staring at me and our eyes locked again. I smiled and didn't disturb their pool game any further. When I caught Shaun staring at me a third time, and our eyes seemed to lock a little longer each time, I decided I would go in for the kill. I sauntered over at the perfect moment and pinched him to get his attention. He jerked upward and I noticed his face was flashing with the same flirtatious spirit. "Hey," I said. "If there's a slow song later, will you dance with me?" He replied that he would with the sweetest country drawl I had ever heard. My knees went weak. I told him that I would request a slow song and that when he heard it, that would be our cue.

When I heard the song come on, I was off chatting with other friends. I had a perfect view of Shaun but he could not see me. I thought I would see just what his reaction would be once he realized this was our intended song. Would he even remember? Would he even care? I got a little nervous as I tested my little theory. I saw Shaun's head jerk up quickly from his pool shot. He then looked quickly to our table and noticing I wasn't there, he scanned the crowd, looking nervously from side to side. My heart quickened. I couldn't believe what I was witnessing, and it was adorable for this guy almost seemed desperate to find me. My test had proved that I was even crazier for this boy. How sweet and honourable he seemed, looking for his lady whom he had promised to dance with. I casually came out of hiding and sauntered in his direction. Soon we were on the dance floor. In the span of two love songs, he knew everything that he needed to know about me. He listened and I loved being wrapped in his strong arms.

When it came time to leave, Shaun approached me and asked for my phone number. I was all smiles for no one had ever asked me for my number before. I gave him my digits and went home with my friends.

When Shaun and I finally connected we quickly made arrangements for dinner and a movie in Winnipeg. We decided it would be convenient to meet at my parents' house as my parents would be looking after Bailey while we were on our date.

On the day of the date, I was all knots and butterflies. I had picked out the cutest outfit and thought you couldn't go wrong with a nice white top and blue jeans. My mother said to me, "When he comes to pick you up make sure he rings the doorbell." I could tell she was very excited for me and that it was important to her to witness him ringing the doorbell. My father seemed a little annoyed but quiet. I knew that he was happy for me but would never enjoy the fact that I was dating. Bailey was playing with his toys and had been told that Mommy had a date but I wasn't sure if he quite understood. Shaun told me he would be driving his new truck, one that I knew he was very proud of. I was looking out for him at the appointed time. When I saw Shaun's truck coming from the distance, I hollered, "He's coming!" My mother reminded me, "Let him ring the doorbell." I agreed but asked her to ensure that Bailey would not be near the front door. I definitely did not want him to be meeting my little man on the first date.

I decided to quickly check my hair and appearance once more before he arrived at the door. While I was fixing my hair I heard the doorbell and was rounding the corner to answer the door when I heard the bold but polite voice of my son. "Hi, I'm Bailey!" My heart leaped. When I reached the front door, the two of them were shaking hands in a gentleman-like fashion. Shaun looked at my son with a smile on his face and my son had the biggest grin you have ever seen. I gave Bailey a quick goodbye and Shaun and I were on our way.

By the time Shaun dropped me off at the end of the evening, we both agreed that we had a great time. Shaun told me he thought my son was adorable and that he would like to see me again. Later we both admitted that we wished our first date would not have had to end.

Shaun had told me the first night we met that he had finally decided what he wanted to be when he grew up and had just begun to pursue a career as a journeyman electrician. He had also decided to pursue more of a truck-driving career and he was excited about his long-distance trips. My father enjoyed talking with Shaun about trucking since he had spent many years in this career path also. It was nice to see my father actually getting to know Shaun. Mom loved him and was proud that I was dating a guy with such strong character. My siblings liked Shaun and my brothers seemed to click with him instantly.

I couldn't help but think back to the prayer wish list I had prayed for so long. Incredibly Shaun's character seemed to fit this list. He was funny and I enjoyed his sense of humour and enjoyed his sensitive, kind heart. He was easily persuaded to see things my way and I thought I had hit the gold mine. Shaun still lived at home to save money for his college years and he ensured that he only gave me honour. Bailey was important to him and they quickly formed a friendship. We had only been dating for a few weeks when Bailey's fifth birthday arrived and he was so excited to receive a gift from Shaun and his parents. I instantly felt welcome by his parents and felt no judgment for being a single mom. Shaun had only one brother, Stephen, who was a few years older. Stephen and I both worked at McCain Foods and we always had lots to talk about. Stephen bonded very quickly with Bailey and would allow him to get away with almost everything. Shaun's parents owned a farm just south of Portage with a moderate herd of cattle and beautiful horses. There were times when Stephen and Shaun would tackle each other, trying to get the best of each other, while we watched. They were in the middle of one of these wrestling matches when their father walked through the kitchen. Whether he wanted to or not, their father was also invited to try for the heavyweight world championship. Soon all three of them were in a heap on the floor, roaring with laughter.

They were a cozy family and I grew extremely close with Shaun's mother. His father was a true gentleman and had raised his sons with the same character. He loved to tease and had the greatest laugh.

There were challenges to dating a single mother and it did make it difficult that Shaun was a long distance truck driver. This was often excruciating for me as I hated dealing with all life's dilemmas alone. I couldn't wait to share the load with a partner.

I so badly wanted to tell Shaun that I loved him, and six months into the relationship I could hold back no more. Shaun politely received this affirmation and said nothing. Little did I know that when you pray for a gentleman, this is the kind of things that you encounter, for a true gentleman will never say I love you when he doesn't mean it yet. I thought this was ridiculous but I had also loved Shaun from the first time I saw him.

I was extremely jealous as Shaun had as many female friends as he had male friends, and often when we would be going to a social gathering, I would hear the girls scream, "Shaunnie!" This drove me crazy as I thought Shaun could replace me easily. My insecurity and neediness took its toll on Shaun and he stated clearly one evening that he wanted to take a little break. I had felt this coming but I was devastated at this reality that it had come to this. He was sick of me and needed time away from me, I would tell myself. The other problem was that, although we both had rich social lives, Shaun somehow seemed to want both the single life and our relationship when it was convenient for him. Dating a single mother brought on a lot of stresses.

We actually had a few of these breakups before I became irritated and decided to play my own games. When my cousin called to tell me Shaun was at a night club, I decided that I would make an appearance. I dolled up and drove to the bar. I was very nervous as I had not seen Shaun for a couple of weeks. I spotted him beside the bar with a group of friends. I saw where my friends were and that I could easily enter the atmosphere of the club without Shaun thinking I had seen him. I wanted to make it look like I was just popping in to say hello to my friends and then heading home. I left the bar and walked back to my car. A newfound sadness washed over me when I told myself that this had been a bad idea. All of a sudden I heard quick-sounding footsteps behind me. They were definitely the sound of cowboy boots, the only footwear Shaun ever wore. My heart jumped and I held my breath for I dared not turn around. I just kept walking towards my vehicle, maybe with a little more wiggle in my hips. I heard someone calling and I slowly turned around. My plan had worked perfectly. We decided to work things out and were on the mend once again.

Things might have been better for Shaun and me, but stresses were adding up for my family. I had been so consumed with my love life that I didn't really understand that life wasn't so easy for Mom and the siblings who still lived at home. My dad had become much more volatile and my siblings were not coping with Dad very well anymore. The stress was getting to a new level. Mom seemed strained but was still trying to be supportive. My father had begun to be more authoritive with my little brother Elias. Dad was unpredictable a lot of the times as he wanted so desperately to make it through this financial trial. He seemed to be more irritated whenever Bailey and I were over.

All the stresses took its toll on my dating relationship, and eventually it seemed to be over for good. It was very painful for me and took me a long time to get out and about. It was easier for Shaun as he was doing trucking full time, and had begun to take classes at Assiniboine Community College for his electrical journeyman certificate. I would see him occasionally as we passed each other on the main street of Portage and we would politely wave to each other.

I was just coming home from a tanning appointment one Saturday afternoon when I noticed Shaun's truck parked near Tecza Mercury, the local dealership where I had purchased my car. I quickly thought this would be a good time to confirm the part I needed for my steering column. I quickly ran into my basement suite and asked Anna if she could babysit a little longer; she agreed. I had lost five pounds due to the emotions of the breakup six weeks before and I strutted into the dealership smelling like a tropical coconut from the tanning appointment, and wearing a tight pair of new jeans that fit perfectly. I walked right past Shaun as he was talking to one of the dealers, sauntered over to the counter and began discussing the part with mechanics. Shaun was outside by the time I left the dealership and we quickly engaged in an easygoing conversation. It felt good to be near him. He told me I looked good and that he had been scared by the look I had given him that I might hate him now. Assuring him that I did not hate him, we made our goodbyes, and then all of a sudden he turned to me and asked me if I would join him and his family for supper. This was definitely more than I had bargained for. How was I supposed to have dinner with his family? When I told him that I didn't feel comfortable going out for dinner, he tried to persuade me and said his relatives were in from Vancouver and it would be fun. I asked him if he thought it a little weird that he would be inviting his ex-girlfriend to supper. He just shrugged his shoulders like it didn't matter. I declined but said I would hang out with him until his dinner party was ready.

We were just walking around the mall when we ran smack-dab into his parents. I had hoped to avoid the awkward meeting and have Shaun just go to the restaurant alone but now we were being looked at by his parents in a peculiar way. "What the heck you two doing together?" his father asked. His mother added in quickly, "Yeah, Shaunnie, aren't you two broken up?" Shaun rolled his eyes at his mother's sarcastic tone and explained that he had thought he would force me to have dinner with them. I quickly explained that I was busy and that I was just helping Shaun kill time. Shaun's mother smacked him in the arm and asked, "You mean you didn't *invite* her to dinner?" I loved this family very much but was not interested in putting myself in a situation where I would hear that I was his ex-girlfriend. His mom settled it when she grabbed my arm and stated, "Well, I miss you, and you're coming for dinner, and that's that."

I knew instantly that I would like Shaun's Uncle Donald and Aunty Gail but there were definitely some awkward moments over dinner. Shaun's Aunty Gail later said that you could cut the tension with a knife at times. Especially the teasing "so you guys are broken up? but you're spending the day together?" Without missing a beat Shaun replied, "I don't think I really want to date her any more." He had the biggest, goofiest smile on his face. I just shook my head from side to side. "They're always breaking up, these two," Shaun's mom said quickly. It was a nice evening and Shaun confessed later that he was scared that I was going to bolt from the dinner under pressure. Shaun and I excused ourselves early from the dinner date. When saying goodbye, we spent some time talking about Bailey and the fact that he had been asking about Shaun often. I asked if he would like to join us for the July first fireworks and spend some time with us. Shaun said he would try and we said our goodbyes. I was hopeful that this would be a nice evening and couldn't wait to tell Bailey.

On July 1, Bailey and I found the perfect view of the fireworks by the crescent lake. We had a blanket for sitting on and one to wrap ourselves into for warmth, but when Shaun was late, I became sure that he wasn't coming—because Shaun was extremely punctual and he would never be late intentionally. I simply had misread him and maybe he was just trying to be polite and couldn't straight out say no. I wrapped myself and Bailey in the warm blanket and held my son securely in my lap. I whispered in his small ear that we would have fun no matter what. I took one more look down the long bank to the west and was shocked to see Shaun in the distance in a full jog running towards us. I whispered to Bailey, "Hey, look who's coming." Bailey gasped and screamed, "Shaun!" The rest of the evening was magical and I don't know what was filled with more majestic sparks, the lit-up sky or the ones flying between us. It was very clear we cared for each other deeply. He apologized for being late and handed me a shiny small golden box. It was from his mother. Inside were three chocolates and a sweet note stating that she was so thankful to have had me join them and that it had made the dinner very special to have had me to introduce. My heart was filled with love and I knew we were together again.

10 FAMILY STRESSES

AS SHAUN AND I TALKED ABOUT OUR LIFE GOALS I TOLD HIM I HAD HAD A DREAM OF being a nurse but I thought I wasn't smart enough for the challenge. Shaun shocked me when he said, "That's the stupidest thing I ever heard!" I just stared at him, stunned. Did he think that I could actually succeed at college? I had longed for an opportunity like this. Without any further thought, the very next day I called the college in Brandon and got all the information I needed for the entrance exam which was scheduled for late February

We spent a romantic New Year's Eve together at the Rumancik farm, with Bailey. The next day we enjoyed a waffle brunch and spent the day skidooing. Bailey, Shaun and I had a blast and ended the day off with Shaun's mom's classic lasagna dinner.

The next day my parents came in to my apartment and although we enjoyed a nice family dinner, I could feel tensions in the air for things were not well. My parents had to make some very hard decisions regarding their financial future and they had come up with a plan that they would both work together on.

In late February, I went into Brandon to write the entrance exam. My cousin Samantha was also thinking of pursuing this career path. As she put it, we would write the exam and then wait for a reply that stated we were intelligent enough to enter into the nursing school. We had some good laughs and I was glad I had her with me to take those first steps. We wrote the three-hour exam and then released it to wait for what would be our outcome.

The very next day, everything I had ever known came crashing down. Reality set in that this was no little family crisis when my mother and sister arrived to stay with us. My father was in a complete manic state and it was clear it was not going to settle overnight. We didn't realize what was going on but I can tell you with most certainty that there was a trigger to my father's manic state, one that we would not understand fully for several years. My mother was completely in emotional pieces as my father, in the beginning states of mania, had told others private details of their marriage. I sat stunned: why would my father do this? We were all in a state of shock and disbelief.

My mother began to fear my father, and she and my sister took an apartment to be safer. My father was enraged when he couldn't undo decisions he had made, which only took his cycle of self-destruction further. I felt it unsafe for Bailey to spend time with my father since he talked in an erratic manner most of the time—and so at the tender age of six, Bailey lost his favourite person in the world. My mother was just trying to come to terms with how my father's anger could turn to a rage that didn't seem to have an end. My brothers and I did everything we could to support both our mother and father, but soon had no options but to avoid contact with our father. At sixteen, my little sister was in a very vulnerable state and had to help Mom financially with her after-school job. We all did our best to support each other. As with any mental illness, people suffering tend to become isolated because they push away all those who could be a support.

My father began to express a hatred for Shaun and this was most difficult for Shaun as he definitely didn't deserve it. Shaun became more of a support with Bailey as he felt broken-hearted for a little man who didn't understand what was happening.

My father got kicked out of restaurants and the RCMP were called a few times to deal with him. His rage was endless. My father had a lot of friends but they were all as confused as we were. There seemed no end to his manic decision-making. He would go to auction sales to purchase goods to try and get my mother to talk to him but to no avail—it would never work. My father had done so many irrational things that she began to fear what he could be capable of next.

My mother had the support of our home church and the new minister. The minister tried to care for my father and saw him as a man of faith. I can verify this, for in all my life I have never seen or heard my father forsake or blame God for anything. I have memories of him sitting at the kitchen table with his Bible open. He loved to pray for people and saw Jesus as his closest friend. My father was the one who would kneel with us every night before bed and recite the Lord's Prayer, usually in German. I loved hearing him read his Bible out loud. My father believed in prayer and in the power of the anointed blood of Jesus. He raised us to know God and to honour His written word.

But when someone has a manic breakdown or suffers from any mental illness, they very often develop a warped sense of religion. We began seeing this in my father as he desperately was trying to get his life on track: he would find verses on forgiveness and marriage, trying to do whatever he could to convince my mother to reconcile. This was not going to work as my mother's fear turned to bitterness and then to hardened pride. It also was not a good thing that our large family seemed to enjoy the latest facts of Dad's life. I was sick of everyone's need to keep up to date with all these sad details of my father's life falling to pieces. Too many people talking and not enough people praying is what I thought.

My brother Conrad was still living at home with my father and definitely verified that things were getting worse. My brother finally had to move out to avoid any further unpredictable actions from my father. Financially, things were very serious and as the pressures of life caved in further on Dad so did his rage. My father was a very creative man and he tried so desperately to keep from having to lose all he owned.

This manic breakdown of my father's lasted over a year and ended with my parents getting divorced and my mother having to completely start over after twenty-five years of marriage.

With all of these new life trials surrounding my immediate family at the same time as I was accepted into the nursing program, Shaun very quickly jumped in to be supportive, picking up Bailey from school on days when I was doing courses, for instance. One of these times Shaun witnessed something very adorable and innocent. Shaun overheard part of a conversation Bailey was having with a few other boys from his class about their dads. He was curious to see what Bailey would say as he listened to all of his classmates obviously bragging about their dads. He was shocked when heard this bold little voice say, "Oh yeah, my dad has a big new truck and a skidoo and he lets me ride it and we do lots of stuff together…" Shaun said he was stunned at the little man speaking about him. Of course the boys wasted no time telling Bailey that he was lying, so Shaun rounded the corner, gave Bailey a big smile and rescued him from the awkward situation.

I started to attend church again with my mother and Bailey at a new church. I enjoyed being back in this atmosphere and found the church to be very friendly but I had no spiritual connection with God as I had walked away from my faith. It made Bailey happy to have me with him. My Uncle Steve and Aunt Sara, who had also left the colony by this time, were also attending the same church. They were very excited for my nursing endeavour and wanted success for me. One day, my Uncle Steve leaned over the pew and said to me, "I hear you got 96% on your test last week." I beamed a huge smile his way and nodded. Without missing a beat, my uncle handed me a piece of paper. I opened it and saw that it was a cheque for ninety-six dollars. I looked up in surprise and was met with a smile from Uncle Steve and a wink from my Aunty Sara. I was so touched by this gift. My uncle said, "Keep up the good work!" My heart was overjoyed.

11
HITTING ROCK BOTTOM

RUNNING OUT TO MY CAR, I KNEW IF I DIDN'T HURRY I WOULD BE LATE FOR MY HAIR appointment. The sun was warm and felt even warmer with the help of my heartbeat. My father had once again been calling all morning and I was extremely frustrated and had hung up on him. I placed my head on the steering wheel, tears starting to come. Oh, how I wished my mother would speak to my father. I had just found out that my parents had agreed that after a few months of separation, they would get together and talk. My father expected my mother to comply with this verbal agreement. She refused, for fear and bitterness had completely closed her off from my father. It was my mother who was now building walls. My father was now increasing the pressure on me to get him access to Mom. Dad was very persistent and I couldn't help but think that my father and I had never been close and now he was so desperately asking if I could have coffee with him and give him any advice on how to convince Mom to talk to him. I had enough to deal with as my own relationship was suffering under all of this pressure.

I met Shaun uptown after my hair appointment and he told me he had a work trip planned to Iowa, that he wouldn't be home for almost a week. Thinking what the week ahead would bring for me, I very quickly saw an opportunity to go with Shaun for it was exactly what the two of us needed. Since Bailey was in full time school it was very easy for Mom to manage her work schedule around him. It was perfect timing since my upgrading courses were complete and I wasn't due to start my human anatomy courses yet.

Soon I was climbing into the front seat and was all smiles. I loved road trips and I was ecstatic for this trip to start. We would be gone for a week and even making a stop in Chicago. It wasn't long before Shaun stopped at our favourite truck stop; he purchased me a few new novels and some saltwater taffy. I loved reading to Shaun aloud and he also enjoyed the entertainment. He wasn't much of a talker and I was, so a perfect compromise was to buy me a book.

Construction on the road delayed us a few hours and we reached the lumberyard just at closing time. Shaun had to bribe the employees who were left to still unload us. As torrential rain began to pour, I went out and decided to help wherever I could. Shaun was quite stressed and now was not looking forward to cleaning up all the tarp straps in the mud. He snapped some rude impatient comments my way and I began to regret coming. Since I was a little girl, I had been used to this kind of stress-filled anger. I just quietly did my best to stay out of his way. I found my own strap to wind up and worked at it as best I could. Then, Shaun came behind me and said he was sorry for being rude. I definitely was not interested in feeling his wet face on my neck, and shivers ran down my arms. We solved our conflict in a rather muddy, rain-filled kiss. It was really hard for me to usually let loose and just have fun but on this trip we had hours of fun. This was just what we needed to relax and rejuvenate ourselves before returning to the war zone that waited for us at home

We had been together for a year and a half by the fall of 2001 and one of our challenges was that Shaun's parents were often very irritated with my son, something that I found very hurtful. Shaun and his brother had been for the most part very compliant children and my Bailey was more unsettled. My fear-based approach parenting definitely didn't help either, for I simply turned up the strictness on my son and kept him on a tight form of discipline, thanks again to the fear of losing control. I was always working to make sure Bailey looked good and acted well.

I started my evening Human Anatomy course and this meant even more time apart from my son. I missed him terribly. Because of shift work and Tuesday/Thursday evening classes in Brandon, I would not see him for two or three days at a time. My father had calmed down some and we had enjoyed some good visits but I was caught between my parents and, having made a vow so long before to be mature, I took it all on my shoulders. Shaun was back in school for four months, too, and I could see him only when attending the evening classes.

My nerves were beginning to wear thin when I joined my mom for breakfast. I peeked in on Bailey who was still sleeping and couldn't resist kissing his soft cheeks. As Mom poured me a cup of coffee, I couldn't help but notice that Mom's life was so calm without Dad's outbursts and I was torn with emotions. Would it be better if they remained separated or reconciled? The weight of the world seemed on my shoulders.

My father had also been in the hospital for a few days with a kidney infection and it was becoming clear that his lifestyle was beginning to take a toll on his physical health. My brothers and I checked to see if he needed anything but my little sister went nowhere near him, which also broke Dad's heart. My mother and sister were doing all they could to stay away from my father.

I was dusting the front room one morning and had the TV on when the screen showed an airplane crashing into a skyscraper. The rest of the morning was spent in horror listening and watching all that happened that fatal day. When I met with Shaun for supper, he confirmed that his classes were barely functional with the world's events swirling around the campus. It was an eerie day as if our world had changed in some huge way. None of us could make sense of any of it. It was all I thought about on my way to college that evening for my first class. It only added to the sense of stress I felt along with my fear of failure. I simply felt I could take no more.

And then it got worse. I had gone to church and Bailey was driving me crazy. He did nothing but act out in church and I was not impressed. Later that day Shaun's mother, Judy, and I were running errands in town and had to stop by my mother's place. I don't recall the exact events but I know that none of us were in agreement on how to handle Bailey. When Bailey decided to bolt away from me, Judy had had enough. She slapped him. We were all stunned but my sister didn't miss a beat and she gave Judy a mouthful. It was a state of complete awkwardness as the whole scene erupted. We tried to deal with the situation as best we could but the damage was great. A lot of lines were crossed and I was very upset that Shaun's mother had hit my son even if Bailey was acting out.

Later, I was on the phone discussing the ordeal with Shaun. He felt like my family chaos had now spilled over into his family, and he made it quite clear that this was more than he could handle. We were discussing the need to break things off when a knock came at the door. I wasn't sure who it was but I was in no rush to get off the phone. I reached for the door. It was my father, asking if he could come in. I told him it wasn't a good time. He asked if he could come back later and if I could help him with something. I was losing patience quickly and felt like I couldn't breathe. I told my father that I probably couldn't make time that day but he persisted to tell me that he wanted my help to write a love letter to Mom. I froze with my hand still holding the phone. I saw the vulnerability in my father's eyes, the tender manner in his expression that showed how he was desperate to get his words to Mom. But I knew there was no way my mother would receive the letter. I let anger take over as I reacted to my father's request.

I lost all control and tears were pouring down my face. I ended my phone call with Shaun but not before he knew I was at the end of my rope. I yelled no to my father as he pleaded. I could not help him and I wouldn't even try for I knew it was a useless attempt. As I sit here now I wish I could go back there and tell myself to get a grip, to write the note with my dad, but I was undone and I couldn't go on. I hovered in a corner and cried as I hung on to my hair, desperate for all this pressure to go away. I didn't have what it took to bear this load. My father, my mother, my son, my relationship with Shaun, my school courses, work, trying to keep the family harmonized. I completely snapped.

My mother came over and she asked me if she could call the pastor. I couldn't make a decision so she called him anyway. I was inconsolable. Shaun arrived with Chasie, his black Lab. I couldn't get the image out of my mind of my father's vulnerable sad eyes with their desperate plea. I had no idea which decision was right or wrong. When the pastor arrived, we all sat around the kitchen table. The pastor asked if he could pray.

As we all bowed our heads, I had no idea that what would happen next would change my life forever. Pastor Dave spoke to me in a matter-of-fact sort of manner. "You've got nowhere to go but up," he said. I will never forget his words and explanation. He told me that I needed to put God first, and that the pressures I was placing on a boyfriend were pressures that only God could carry.

I then interrupted him by saying that I was nowhere near ready to commit to God again as I had too many wrong issues to let go of. What he said next blasted any lies that ever formed in my heart. "We don't need to carry around a spiritual checklist and make sure we do not swear, do not drink, dance, smoke or sin…" He told me that Jesus wanted me just the way I was, and that with His help I could attain anything. Jesus is not interested in a perfect being; He's interested in that person loving Him the most. Once I had a personal relationship with Jesus, he said, I would thrive. He asked me if I was interested in this perfect opportunity. I felt different. I understood the point of Jesus and I accepted. I can tell you that this was a humbling experience, for here I was sitting with my boyfriend who I had met in a bar, and with a minister, and I had just had a nervous breakdown.

I feel with my whole heart that humility is the greatest key to coming to Jesus. He doesn't need strong people to come to Him—He needs people to be strong because of Him. I finally got it! I accepted the offer to pray and dedicated my life back to Jesus. I had discovered the perfect truth of God's grace. I felt a peace I had never felt before, for it was mixed with an understanding that would hold my faith forever. Jesus is the key to true joy and only through a relationship with Him would I achieve all my dreams, including becoming a nurse.

I was so thankful that my mother had phoned her minister and that she had helped create my godly intervention. As my mother later hugged me, I told her how overwhelmed I felt with her and my father's separation, and Dad's determined manner to show that he cared. She made it very clear to me that it would never be my responsibility to orchestrate a reconciliation between her and Dad. I nodded in agreement and felt I could be free to just try and take care of myself and my son.

My Aunty Sara was soon at my side to wrap her arms around me and tell me she was proud I had found my faith, that I was a good mother, that Shaun was an incredible guy—that any man who could endure what he had to face in our family was a man worth waiting for. She encouraged me to give Shaun the space he needed. I agreed.

My next evening class, Shaun was waiting. He had gone back to Brandon after our chat with the minister. I had not seen him since that afternoon with the minister. I was still beaming when I walked up to him and wrapped my arms around his neck. I told him that I wanted him in my life but I no longer needed him for my only need was to love God first. I could feel God's amazing love in my heart and it felt wonderful. Shaun noticed this newfound confidence and told me later it was then that he fell in love with me. I had it figured out and had the inner strength to walk by faith.

I had a good talk with my father and told him that I was sorry I had over-reacted. I told my father of my decision to have faith in Jesus again and he was glad.

Life was not giving Dad any breaks as far as Mom was concerned and their separation took them to court. My father was devastated and still couldn't seem to pull his life together without her. He was angry at this for he could find no way to resolve this mess. His actions just pushed her farther away like it was a well-rehearsed cycle. I ran into my father after court and he looked awful. I gave him a hug and told him I loved him. My father and I by no means had a perfect relationship but it was on its way to being better. My faith in God was moulding me into becoming an honourable daughter. There were many days when I acted no better than my father but we kept looking up.

Bailey was happy to sit with me in church and as I looked around at all the people in church, I leaned over to Mom, "Everyone looks so different now." "No," my mother replied, "It is you that's different." I knew what she meant.

These were many of the same people who had been in this church since I was a little girl and I had never understood how they could sing and pray in adoration for God. Yes, I know we are told to in the Bible but now I too adored my Jesus and knew in my heart it was all about Him. I didn't need the right song to praise or the right words to pray, for I had Him in the right place in my heart and that was the key.

12 BUILDING UP FAITH WHILE FACING FAILURES

MY FOCUS HAD COMPLETELY SHIFTED. I KNEW WHAT I NEEDED TO SUCCEED IN THIS journey I was on. I would accomplish my goals even in the face of failure, even when the road looked empty. I believed that *"I can do everything through Christ who gives me strength"* (Philippians 4:13, NLT).

Attending church regularly and meeting with the pastor, I grabbed hold of all I could to persevere, for I was far from perfect but I was desperate to succeed. I still had a lot of sinful habits like anger, cursing, smoking and loving the night life. I am in no way condemning people who live with these things but can testify that I needed Jesus every moment of every day to try to live a whole life. The peace and faith I had was wonderful and I didn't feel alone anymore. I began to learn that it was not my responsibility to keep my family together and that only God could accomplish most of the things I was trying to fix.

My evening courses still continued and I worked hard. My father was able to spend time with Bailey while I studied and Shaun on occasion helped me study the more challenging parts, like the names of bones and muscles. Time moved very quickly and Christmas was upon us. It would be our first Christmas with my parents separated. It was hard but we made it through. I did not pass my evening class and I was overwhelmed with sadness but I convinced myself that I would at least now know what to expect in the nursing program and told myself that success was not about whether or not I passed but that I still persevered to the goal ahead. My prize was to be crowned with the title of nurse. So with my acceptance letter in hand, I began preparing for the July 2002 intake.

It was becoming clear to Shaun that our relationship was wavering and he was not looking forward to being apart for the whole nursing program. He was completing his apprenticeship final level the following year and was becoming more focused on his career path. Dating a single mom meant he couldn't just be this free spirit. I had my faith and was very much heartbroken. After all we had been through, how could this guy break up with me just as I was starting nursing school? He made it clear that he would move me to Brandon and ensure that I was completely settled before we would part ways. We had found an apartment right near the college and there was a home daycare right across the parking lot. Bailey and I had everything within walking distance. Most people could not imagine going to nursing school with a child in tow but I could never imagine having gone through this time without my son. He was only eight but was incredibly independent. For the hardest part of the course it was Bailey who took care of me.

I studied for hours but I missed the mark most of the time, lacking study skills and having a fear of a failure. And then, a few weeks into the course, Shaun made it known that he was very clear about us breaking up. I realized I had absolutely no choice but to let Shaun go

By mid-September, Bailey and I had found a nice routine (or as Bailey recollects it, we were living on homemade fried rice. I would just cook up enough for the week and then warm-ups it was.) I worked hard at trying to be organized so I could thrive in class. Bailey was the one who got himself up for school, made himself breakfast and ran over to the sitters before school. I often had later classes and studied until two or three a.m. with my study group (Kym, Shirlee and Trish), and so I was thankful for my independent little man. He showed amazing maturity at such a young age. Bailey and I knew we were a team but he did not take it well when I explained to him that Mom and Shaun's relationship was over. Shaun had promised Bailey that they would still do their Boys Only stuff and I kept explaining that the only difference would be that Mom would not be in the picture. Shaun would always be in Bailey's life. Bailey so deserved a good man in his life and as convinced as I had been that it was Shaun, I also had to let the reality of what I told him sink into my heart.

I put all my energy into my studies and thanks to my newfound friends began to smile again. We had a lot of fun with our many role plays in class and made many lasting memories. I loved my class and found a lot of classmates who shared my faith. I enjoyed our theology discussions based on the Bible truths that I had overlooked all my life. I began to see that every good gift came from God and He was very present in my educational endeavour. There was all I needed right there in front of me and my confidence blossomed once again. I was indeed a child of the most high God, single mother and college nursing student.

My father had to walk away from everything, and he moved back to our former Hutterite colony. This is also not common—you don't easily move back to a colony, but here again blood ties proved stronger than religion. My father's brothers and his parents took him in with open arms and helped him regain his life. I enjoyed my relationship with my father and there were more good days than bad. My mother still wouldn't speak to my father, and my father, still desperate for my mother, just took it day by day. His oldest brother had passed away a few years earlier and my father's presence was good for his nephews who were missing their father. Being back at Pinecreek was the start of his healing journey coming full circle in God's provision. My Uncle Steve and Aunt Sara were very much involved in my college years and made it very clear that they daily prayed "that Jenny would pass all of her tests." Yes, I still had two names, in nursing school I was Susan, and in my family, I was Jenny. I knew and felt the power of people's prayers. I can guarantee that I would never have passed theory in college had it not been for my faith.

It was end of September and I was working on an assignment. Bailey had been playing upstairs with his Lego and I wondered if maybe he had fallen asleep. I slowly crept upstairs to our rooms. I was surprised to hear country music. My father had purchased Bailey a stereo and he had been excited but hadn't used it that often. Bailey was sitting cross-legged on the floor with something in his hand. I looked closely and noticed that it was a framed picture of Shaun, Bailey and me. I was shocked when I heard Bailey sniffle. I quietly walked into his room, swept him into my arms and rocked him to the tune of the song. He poured out his heart when I apologized for his hurting little heart. I asked him if he would like to see Shaun and we agreed that I would arrange for them to hang out soon. I acknowledged that I would not be able to go with them but that I was sure Shaun missed him too.

Shaun and I had not spoken in nearly two months and I was convinced that it was over between us and felt I had released him. I had moved on and enjoyed feeling the sunshine in my heart again. I was making the phone call on behalf of a little boy who loved and missed Shaun and was definitely entitled to see him again. I felt nervous calling Shaun, not knowing where life had led him but I took a deep breath and decided to make the phone call while Bailey was playing within earshot. I would call him to the phone once I had discussed with Shaun the reason for my call. I rehearsed my speech like a complete nervous twit. When he answered, his voice sent my heart pounding. We made simple chit-chat and I made it very clear that I was not manipulating anything but simply phoning on

Bailey's behalf. I felt good and confident in stating this truth; I was delighted to realize that I had gained some inner strength. I told Shaun of the incident where Bailey was holding his picture. Shaun thought it was adorable, as he always had a soft spot for Bailey's heart. I called Bailey to the phone and he was all smiles when he recognized his voice on the other end. Shaun agreed that he could come to see Bailey and we arranged for Shaun to come in the next few days. I would make dinner for the two of them and then let them have some alone time. We said our goodbyes and I felt good hanging up the phone. I stood a moment longer by the phone and rubbed the back of my neck. So this was how it felt to be stronger and not to be all crazy with emotions. I felt like I truly would be okay being single. I had achieved life without Shaun. I still had some things to finish up for Monday's classes and went about to accomplish them.

Bailey was playing outside when I noticed Shaun pull up. I went outside and watched Bailey run over to greet him. I thought that he would have been stuck like glue to Shaun for hours but after about thirty minutes Bailey proved he was more interested in his friends and ran off to play. It felt awkward to see Shaun again. I apologized quickly and told him that, honestly, Bailey had been the whole motive behind my phone call. Shaun acted like he was not concerned with my explanation and said he was thinking of coming to check on us anyways, which surprised me greatly. Shaun and I spent the entire evening together. We definitely had not lost the spark and the reality hit hard as he drove away that evening how much I had missed him. Bailey and Shaun made plans to go hang out soon and he was all smiles as we stood waving goodbye. He was getting ready to move to Brandon for his last level of journeyman training in mid-October and had assured Bailey they would see each other lots.

As I walked to class the next day with my friend Shirlee, I told her of the visit. She had watched me go from tears to strength in the last two months. We got to class and settled into the routine of the day. When I returned home, I unlocked my door, welcomed the cool air of the apartment, and grabbed the mail. I noticed a hand-written envelope with a Portage return address. It was from Shaun! I sat down quickly and couldn't believe what I was reading. Every girl would love to hear a guy say what Shaun had written to me. I still have the letter and have read it over and over again. He stated that the summer months had left him wallowing around the farm, completely lost and miserable. He thought that he had given our relationship a fair enough go but that it was the right thing to end it. It didn't take him but a few weeks into our break-up before he had realized that his world was completely empty without Bailey and me in it; he found his days meaningless if he didn't have them to share with me. He had been desperate to call me many times and every time he went to pick up the phone to dial he didn't go through with it. I couldn't believe what I was reading.

What was even crazier was that the date on the letter and envelope proved he had written and mailed the letter before I had even called him. At the bottom of the letter, he asked if we could talk sometime, that he would like us back in his life again if it wasn't too late. There under his signature was his phone number, like I didn't know it. I don't think my feet touched the ground.

I called him right away. He was serious about his commitment and wanted to be together again. I felt like I just received a double dose of everything I had ever longed in a relationship. Yes indeed, he was the man I had prayed for so long ago. God was faithful!

In my course, I was enjoying learning about mental health and could see where my father's triggers were and how difficult it was for someone to be successful at managing a mental illness without a strong support system. My mother had done this well for twenty-five years and I could see why she was bitter and burned out. My father was still living in Pinecreek which gave us the opportunity to visit on occasion. It was nice to get to know my grandparents better since my father was staying with them. I got to know my grandmother Rachel's spiritual side and was in awe of her intercessory gifts. (Before this time, my main memory of this grandmother was of making buns with her. I remember bun baking day and how all her little granddaughters would watch her elegant hands and stern instructions on just what to do to get the best dinner roll. When she would toss perfectly shaped chunks of dough our way, we would begin that perfect half-cupped hand roll. We knew when Grandma thought we had achieved her perfection for she would soon toss us a second chunk of dough, one for each little hand.) I often think how God works all things for good and this was definitely a season that I enjoyed. The few years that Dad stayed there were ones that I will always cherish.

Things were beginning to get more difficult for Bailey at school, though, as his teacher was concerned about his ability to focus. She found him to be increasingly disruptive in her class and he wasn't getting along with his classmates.

I was feeling overwhelmed with my course load and an instructor who seemed to have it in for me. It was no secret that instructors were always looking to see where a person was not suited for the nursing role. You could be as smart as you wanted to be but it all came together at the practicum level. I wanted to be a nurse more than anything else but my fear sometimes left me as a babbling fool.

I was all chatter and this instructor took notice. She took the little confidence I had and trashed it. It was not her fault that I was bound by anxiety and fear; she simply noted that I was so overwhelmed at the practical level that I couldn't even think straight. The reality hit me hard that I would not be passing my term two practicum and my friends were also in shock. We were a tight group and were often told our class was unique and fun. I couldn't imagine leaving behind my study group for we were very close. My heart was ripped apart just thinking of saying goodbye and not getting to graduate with them. My college instructors told me there was a Licensed Practical Nuse (LPN) nursing course through the aboriginal northern communities being held in Portage and that I could re-do my term two practicum experience with them as they were halfway through the program and were accepting non-aboriginal students. So instead of graduating in October, I would graduate in December of the same year. It seemed to be exactly what Bailey and I needed, to move home to Portage and continue my nursing right at home. I was very excited. It seemed like all the doors were opening wide open. As I battled with the remnants of my fear of failure, once again I felt God's reassurance whisper the truth. I had not failed because of academics; I had not failed because of theory. I had definitely not failed because of my character. I only had to redo a two-week practicum. I grabbed on to this new truth and shoved my fear of failure to the ground, crushing it like you would a cigarette butt! In order for us to face our fears, we often have to walk through the heat of them. I was *not* a failure for I was determined to march ahead to earn the prize and become the nurse I so desperately wanted to be.

13 SUSAN RUMANCIK OR JENNY RUMANCIK?

THANKFUL FOR GOD'S PROVISION, IN THE SPRING OF 2003, BAILEY AND I MOVED BACK home to Portage. Bailey was able to join in with his former classmates and with a teacher we absolutely adored. My father was settled into his life back in Pinecreek and was a welcome help. My mother and siblings were doing well and my little sister was getting ready for her grade twelve graduation.

Shaun wanted to purchase his first home so that Bailey and I would have a place to live. An opportunity fell into place very quickly and he put in a bid. His offer was accepted and Bailey and I settled in. There was one problem, or at least I felt it was a problem. Since Shaun had purchased the house for Bailey and I to rent, he decided that he would take this opportunity to move in with us. We had been together for long enough and he thought it was time. Of course I wanted it too but felt convicted instantly. Having just made a new commitment to my faith, I took Jesus' teachings very seriously. I definitely did not want to live common-law, but there was no way I could tell Shaun he could not move in with us. Feeling like I was caught between a rock and a hard place, I pushed my emotions aside.

Shaun and I had a lot of conversations about our future and his belief in God. He definitely believed and had been brought up in the church but was not as zealous as I was. I had been attending church frequently and he had come with Bailey and me. We were attending the same church my parents had brought me to as a child. Mom enjoyed having us with her in worship. Mom had told me that being a divorced woman had felt awful and it was a level of aloneness she couldn't explain easily but said that she felt she didn't fit in anywhere in the world. I tried to imagine but couldn't and was glad to be with her again.

With my term-two practicum behind me, I was enjoying all the new theory that term three brought. It is known as the hardest level of nursing and I had been nervous about the undertaking. Astonishingly I discovered that my study skills were working, and I thrived academically, with a newfound confidence. I grew to love my classmates very quickly—the group of aboriginal girls were from northern communities so remote that you could reach them only by air. They had left all their families and loved ones behind and were all alone in the Portage area. I was in awe of the courage this took. There is definitely a connection I will always have with the aboriginal people; I absolutely love their authentic spirits. Their down-to-earth nature was a welcome addition to my nursing class and I loved their authentic personalities. Our class was a small group so we got to know our instructors closely. I loved class and my marks soared.

At the same time, I was becoming more and more convicted about the guilt of living with Shaun before marriage. We had conversations about when we would get married, the cost, the saving of money to afford the wedding. The list went on and on. I was desperate for a solution but there seemed to not be an easy one. Shaun had finally finished his schooling and was working for a local electrical company, Point West Electrical. He loved his job and enjoyed getting to know his new boss. Talking about weddings only brought about more arguments as I wanted to come up with a solution. There seemed to be none. I decided to settle with Shaun committing to more of my faith—at least we could be equally yoked as the Bible would recommend, both committed to living a righteous life and following the same faith. Shaun had his apprehensions with the fact that I attended a Pentecostal church for he had been raised in a Presbyterian church and had heard more than enough stories about the Pentecostal holy rollers. I understood his dilemma and came up with a great idea. I would call our pastor over for coffee and Shaun would then be free to ask him all the questions he wanted. Shaun agreed and the minister was penciled in for coffee at our place.

Pastor Dave came over on the afternoon of Saturday June 21. Shaun and the minister engaged in conversation easily but somewhere in the conversation the topic turned into our present circumstances and what Pastor Dave said sent shock waves into my already convicted being. "Susan, how can you be a professing Christian and still be living with your boyfriend in sin? My problem is not whether Shaun lives in sin but you and I both know that you have committed to living for God the right way and now here you are living with your boyfriend."

I sat stunned and began to babble excuses of all sorts. Pastor Dave simply stated that living for God has many blessings and many rewards but we have to understand that God expects us to work hard at seeking his wisdom and direction and to not just do life our way when it suits us better. He understood that we had a dilemma but knew that God had a way for us to accomplish it without living together before we were married. The whole reprimand was pointed at me and I was stunned. He made it very clear that even though Shaun was also living in sin, he had not yet made a decision to follow Christ but I *had*.

I had not seen this coming, and after Pastor Dave left you can imagine the argument that Shaun and I had. It was clear to both of us that we could not leave this issue unresolved any longer. When all the angry words I had in my heart had caught air, although I was both embarrassed that Pastor Dave had seemingly only blamed me for our common-law arrangement, and angered that it was solely up to me to stand for my faith, I realized he was right. This minister saved me from guilt and condemnation with the godly truth. I calmly looked at Shaun and told him that the best thing to do for me was to pack up Bailey and myself, and find a small apartment. Shaun's eyes flashed with passion as he said, "You're not taking my son and moving to an apartment. These last few months have been the happiest I have ever been!" Shaun had never referred to Bailey as his son before and he usually didn't speak with such passion. I liked it. "Your son?" I asked. Shaun didn't change his facial expression so I told him, "Listen, honey, those are marrying words" Shaun wasn't backing down and, with a flirtatious smile, said, "Well, let's get married on Friday!" I thought for a second, and replied, "Okay!" He panicked a little but I said, "Why not get married on Friday? I think it's a good idea. But why don't you head to the farm, grab your horse and go take a ride through the pasture while you think it over." He looked at me in disbelief but couldn't argue with the fact that a horseback ride would be exactly what he needed. We made plans to meet up later.

As these new ideas whirled around my head I couldn't help but think I was crazy, but couldn't come up with a good enough reason to why we couldn't just get hitched. As I drove out to meet Shaun at his parents' farm, I felt a peace in my spirit that it would all work out. I found Shaun by the back cattle corrals and we began a heart-to-heart talk that left us both thinking that maybe this wasn't such a bad idea.

We decided that he would phone a Justice of the Peace and see if we could indeed get married on Friday. Why not stick with the original day Shaun had used in his initial comment? As I arrived in class, I quickly told the girls the fact that I might be getting married by the end of the week. I was met with excitement and awe as my classmates loved the love story, especially the part where I told my cowboy boyfriend to saddle the horse and think about it. We were in the heat of term three and had many exams to write that week—I would have exams on the day I was to get married if we went through with our crazy plans.

We told our parents, close friends and relatives. My mother was a little concerned with our timing; she was consumed with my sister's grad ceremonies as it was the end of June. We realized that it would be a busy weekend to get married. My father was ecstatic that we were getting married and Shaun and I enjoyed his enthusiasm. He would be there no matter what. I knew in my heart that many thought I should get my son to walk me down the aisle but I was very determined that my father was the only one that deserved this honour.

After school on Monday, we sat down with Bailey and discussed our plans with him. As he sat and pondered it, Shaun ruffled Bailey's hair and decided that the two of them needed some man time. Shaun informed me later that he asked Bailey if he could marry his mom. Bailey was quick to give him his blessing. I was thankful for a man that would do such an honourable thing for my son, once again confirming the petition to God for a specific man. Check yes for honourable!

We decided that it would only be fair to notify Pastor Dave of our plans and give him the honour of marrying us, if he didn't think we were both crazy. The phone call came as a shock to the minister but he was filled with delight at our decision and that he would consider being a part of our special day if he could meet with us to discuss our plans. We agreed. This time the minister once again had a spiritual blessing for me. He agreed to marry us and encouraged Shaun to consider the option of accepting Jesus into his life. Shaun had been raised in the church and had a good understanding of faith but had never before made a commitment to Christ that was personal. Shaun answered all of his questions and the pastor finished off their talk with this comment, "Do you think this is the woman for you, the woman of your dreams?" Shaun acknowledged that I was indeed the woman that he wanted to marry. The minister then recommended that we equally be in agreement with our faith and asked if Shaun wanted to proclaim that Jesus was indeed the son of God, who was born as a baby on earth, who died on the cross for our sins and who rose again for us to believe he is the Messiah. Shaun agreed and as he held my hand he accepted Jesus as his Saviour. I was so thankful and offered many thanks to God for orchestrating these events in my life. I was overwhelmed. So it was decided that Pastor Dave would be delighted to marry us on Friday June 27 at five p.m., outside, weather permitting.

What about the ring? What about the dress? We headed down to the jewelry store where Shaun picked out a beautiful princess-cut Polar Bear diamond ring.

It was beautiful. Shaun made plans to work weekends to pay off the hefty cost. It had to be sized but it would be ready in time for our wedding. As soon as we finished at the jewelers, we headed to the Forks in Winnipeg, a beautiful getaway near the Assiniboine waterway. We practiced calling each other husband and wife, and joy filled our beings. We reminisced about all the times we had spent in Winnipeg on our many dates and looked forward to many more. As we sat outside Shaun's favourite ice-cream shop, he asked for my hand in marriage.

I had planned to wear a simple white dress that I owned but after trying it on, I knew quickly that it just wouldn't work. I was on the phone with my soon-to-be mother-in-law discussing what to do, when she said, "What about my wedding dress? It's not the prettiest but it's a dress—just try it." So off I went and the dress miraculously fit. I was ecstatic as I ran around the farmhouse, screaming in delight, giving no care or concern to the fact that Shaun, his father, and his brother were my audience.

I was also cramming for my exams on Friday. Shaun had found an old family wedding band that had belonged to his mother's uncle. As I was trying to study in a quiet place, my soon-to-be hubby was doing his best to share all his excitement with me. I had given him every right to wear whatever he wished, for this was a man who took his attire very seriously and I knew I could never persuade him to wear a suit. I was studying when along came Shaun and Bailey again. They had just been shopping and had matching outfits: black suit jackets, white dress shirts, blue jeans, and cowboy boots and they were all smiles. Oh yes, they also had cowboy hats.

During this whirlwind, I decided that it could be a great time to take on my true given identity. As my last name was being changed anyway, I would change my first name legally to Jenny. I was a Jenny in every way and wished I had never been so headstrong in using the name Susan, even if it was my legally given name. I believed it was my destiny to be Jenny and no one understood this more than me. Shaun was not as supportive as I would have liked but then he never embraces change easily. The rest of his family began calling me Jenny instantly and I was grateful for their support. Even my family had found it difficult to know whether to call me Jenny or Susan and they would use both my names in different settings. I was tired of the confusion. My classmates were new enough in my life that they quickly began to call me Jenny too. The decision was made and my birth certificate was changed from Susan to Jenny.

Our wedding day had threats of rain as we quickly made our way to our church. Everything was set: my brother Conrad as the photographer, my friends from college as my maid of honour and master of ceremonies, and Shaun's brother as the best man. We had all we needed. My father came in for the day and we tried as best as we could to get through the day without any issues. My parents had not spoken in a few years so there were definitely emotions under the surface. There were a total of nineteen people at our wedding and we were thankful for the small gathering. We had told all of our friends and family that we were making our vows to God as our witness and would plan a reception on our one-year anniversary. As I drove to the church with my father, he was definitely stressed in seeing my mother, but I reminded him that it was my wedding day and we would make it through. I held my father's arm tightly as I walked down the aisle. I was all smiles as I took my place beside my groom. We said our vows and Shaun was filled with emotion—there it was again, my prayer request for a sensitive man. My face beamed even brighter when he placed my beautiful ring on my finger for the first time. The deal was then sealed with a kiss.

The church had been decorated very elegantly for this Friday evening wedding. All had come together to make it beautiful despite the rain. My son looked sharp in his ringbearer attire and, yes, he perfectly matched the groom. We all headed to our house for a small family gathering and enjoyed the celebration. My parents were civil and it was a complete success. It was final I was the wife of Shaun Rumancik—Jenny Rumancik.

The summer was filled with bliss as we enjoyed camping adventures and our newest addition to our family, our puppy, Charlie Brown. Shaun's work was going well and I was finishing up my LPN course.

With graduation ceremonies and the final exam behind us, we all eagerly waited for the letter that would arrive in the mail officially stating that we had *passed* our nursing exam and could officially call ourselves Licence Practical Nurses. I still remember opening the envelope and with a scream declared it was official: *I was a nurse*. The feeling was overwhelming and my dream was finally achieved. I quickly took on a casual position at our local hospital and put my nursing skills to the test. I loved being a nurse and found that the needle phobia I had had as a child was cured by giving needles. It was my great honour to care for Hutterite patients and use my German as an added skill. I cherished the opportunity to care for these people when they were my patients. God used many of these moments as extraordinary means to validate my true character. As a nurse you are taught to value your integrity and act in an assertive manner and I could be assertive in tough situations with coworkers.

One of our nursing instructors said goodbye to us at the end of our course and gave us a gift and instructions I will never forget. She handed us each a Gideon Bible. It was white and was meant for nurses and she told us that this in our pocket was just as important as any nursing manual we could find. I thought what a perfect opportunity to do the Lord's work—while we could help mend the body, we could nurture the soul. I grabbed hold of that truth.

When I was approached by our church camp to act as camp nurse, I was thrilled. Having spent time there with my family and youth group, I was eager for the chance to return. It was also as close as I could get to colony life. This would also give Bailey the opportunity to go to kids camp and, since I was still an over-protective parent I figured this was perfect, and so it began my career as camp nurse. Little did I know how much I would learn through the years at kids camp. There is always a special anointing at summer camp.

We were enjoying our new congregation and Shaun and I had decided to be baptized together, sealing our commitment to faith. (Hutterites get baptized before the wedding service, sealing their salvation before they are committed to a marriage covenant. We did it in the opposite order but both were important to us.) Preparing for our baptism service, we each wrote out our testimonies. Shaun wrote his down very quickly and his passions were easily put together about how he had grown up in church all his life but had never understood what it meant to have a personal relationship with Jesus. He was serious about this newfound relationship with Jesus. I was encouraged by Shaun's written testimony and began searching my soul. It didn't take me long before my first Scripture memory sang in my heart—like an old tune so long forgotten I quickly remembered the words of Matthew 5:16. I could see very clearly how God had orchestrated my life. I once again confirmed that I desired to be a light for Jesus. I loved Him with all my heart and wanted people to see Jesus in my life. I would definitely need Him to help me grow out of my selfish angry temper.

I made vows as a young bride, thinking I knew it all. I would not be like my mother was, just letting my father rant and curse and cut her to the core. I would also not be like my mother-in-law, who was often not assertive in her marriage but would leave things unsaid. I would speak my mind, stick up for myself, and fight back if need be. I also declared that I would have made a not-so-good Hutterite wife because I did not agree with the idea that men should be served like royal kings. My husband did not argue this matter and readily agreed that he didn't need to be served. He was dependent on no one.

Adjusting to being married is a challenge for any relationship, especially in the first years of marriage when you find out how differently each of you were raised. We had volatile anger in our family, while Shaun's family had lots of sarcasm, both of which are a product of anger. I am so thankful that God placed women in my life to mentor me to be the woman God created me to become. I took a lot of wrong roads but thankfully came to understand that by grace we are saved.

Sunday morning church services gave us lots of insight, and we enjoyed getting to know the ministers and were so thankful they were there in the mentorship for marriage and Christian growth. Pastor Dave encouraged us to take the marriage counselling that is often done prior to a wedding. We agreed and began to learn much about personality types and helpful insights to a healthy marriage.

Shaun and I were approached about teaching a Sunday school class and I was excited to teach children. Shaun and I struggled with teaching as a team but we got some rare glimpses of moments where both of our authentic gifts flowed. I shudder as I think back how immature we were as baby Christians stepping out in ministries. I definitely still had insecurities and couldn't tolerate Shaun's moments of simply poking fun at me. We had a lot of fun with our class teaching them the theology of the Old Testament. It was here where I knew I had a passion for children's ministry. I wanted to tell the kids the truth about God in a way they would remember into their adulthood. I wanted to stir up the hunger for them to want to know God more. Shaun was totally fun with the kids and they adored him. Jesus loved kids and often in crowds when He preached He made sure they were close. During one of these sermons, His disciples told the mothers to watch their children to ensure they didn't disturb the message. Jesus stopped speaking and told them to let the children be and reminded them that we should be more like children. He was an advocate for the genuine spirit of a child. I decided that Jesus would probably rather be in the Sunday School hanging out with the kids than a bunch of adults who sometimes sit too rigidly. I wanted nothing more than to be as near to Jesus as I could get.

We were closer with my father as we enjoyed many good visits with Dad as he still lived in our former colony. He was getting stronger, enjoying his purpose in life and helping the colony thrive. My relatives were so happy for me and could see that Shaun was a good match for me.

One time, we had just arrived and were enjoying the afternoon coffee time when my grandfather made it clear that he was stressed: he had been calling all over to find someone to come fix some lights but both the Hutterite electrician and the electricians in the local towns were booked up. Shaun gave me a weird look and then asked if he could help. My grandfather looked at Shaun, and without an emotion, asked, "What is it you do for a living?" With a chuckle, Shaun told him he was an electrician. The expression on my grandfather's face was priceless. My grandfather continued his excitement as he described all the details of the lights he needed to fix. He stopped and took one more look at Shaun in total disbelief. He placed his hand on Shaun's shoulder and said, "Do you realize how I prayed this morning for God to send me an electrician?" From the look on Shaun's face, I couldn't quite make out whether he was happy or scared to be Grandpa's miracle electrician. It didn't matter because before long Shaun was standing on top of a chair fixing the ceiling light for Grandpa. My grandfather was over the moon with excitement and gave us all a sermon on prayer and miracles. I loved that this was the first time my Shaun got to meet my grandparents. I was so proud.

On our way home Shaun worried that he might kill my grandfather with accidental electrocution as my grandfather had had Shaun rewire an old portable turkey roaster. You didn't say no to my grandfather and when Shaun was giving my grandfather instructions on code and safety, we heard our grandfather's familiar rant, "That doesn't matter. We'll make it work just like this and nothing to worry about!"

With our anniversary wedding reception nearing, it was easy to see why our first year of marriage seems a blur to me. We did everything together, Shaun and me. He definitely was a man with an opinion. With all the details in place, I had even purchased my own wedding dress for the event. Our minister helped Bailey and me arrange a surprise presentation for Shaun set to the song *He Didn't Have to Be* by Brad Paisley, about a man who marries a single mom. Bailey loves that song about a man who was a dad although he didn't have to be. I knew Bailey had wanted to call Shaun "Dad" for a long time but I didn't allow him until we were married. It was awkward at first but helped us feel like a real family. Bailey was aware of who his biological father was but he had had no one to call Dad. Bailey and I knew that Shaun was the dad we had prayed for.

As we arrived at our reception destination, a crowd of my Hutterite relatives greeted me. I was much honoured as it wasn't the norm for Hutterites to attend outside weddings, but I would never dream of not extending an invitation to the ones who had stood by me all my life. The banquet room was filled with guests as Shaun and I entered. It was awkward to enter a reception all decked out in wedding attire when our wedding ceremony had been a whole year prior, but here Shaun's dad took the lead, escorting us into the reception hall, jigging the whole way and proving he was a gentleman both inside and out, as well as showing his fun-loving side. We were thankful to share this day with our 125-plus crowd. Even Shaun's family from Vancouver had flown in for the occasion. We were blessed! As we all moved to the dance area in the adjoining room we showed the Power Point presentation and there wasn't a dry eye in the room.

Our friends and family danced the night away as Bailey lay fast asleep on the sofa, all tuckered out, his cowboy boots close beside him. He had had a full day, especially getting to tell everyone at the appointed time that he soon would be a big brother. We were expecting a baby before the end of the year. It was nice to prove to everyone that our quick wedding the year before had not been a shotgun wedding.

14 THE CUTTING OF APRON STRINGS

WE WERE ALL EXCITED! THIS WAS VERY DIFFERENT THAN BEING A SINGLE MOTHER AND I was looking forward to having a husband by my side through this journey. This would be the first grandchild for Shaun's parents. I loved them dearly but knew their apprehensions about becoming grandparents. It was no secret that Shaun's parents found children irritating.

On November 13, our daughter arrived six weeks early at five pounds. I had wanted a little girl badly. We named her Sadie Jane Rumancik. She was classified as a preemie and we were scheduled to stay in the neonatal unit in Winnipeg for a few weeks. She was a healthy baby but we would stay in the hospital until she gained back her birth weight. This was all new to us and we were thankful to all the friends and family who were near for support. As friends and family came to visit, we knew she would be a much-loved little girl. Having a few aunts and uncles of mine living in the city gave us a great opportunity to get some special visits. The staff in the hospital were very supportive and always encouraged couples to take a break from the hospital. The most precious moment was when Sadie's big brother came to meet her. Bailey was so happy!

I enjoyed getting to know another mother in the unit who had had a little boy around the same time. One day when Shaun was visiting, the father across from us was holding his son and came across the small walkway dividing the unit. We made chit-chat and the dad introduced his little man to Sadie, who was just being bundled up after being changed. Shaun, never missing a moment for humour said, "Aw, Sadie, look, the first boy that saw you without your shirt on." The other dad didn't miss a beat and stated, "My son is a gentleman—he didn't look." We all had a good laugh.

While in the neonatal (NICU) unit, I had some treasured quiet time to enjoy some reading. A friend from church had given me a care package and its contents changed my life forever. She had been in the NICU a few months before and knew just what I would need. In the package, I found a novel that she had stated in her note was her favourite book. I had never heard of this author and I hate to admit that I was not keen on trying new authors. The cover displayed a bold swirl of red and the title was *The Scarlet Thread* by Francine Rivers. I decided that I would give this book a chance. Thank goodness I did! This book not only consumed me but it completely enchanted me with her amazing ability to capture the essence of God at work in a broken marriage, and the wife working on her faith. My little quiet times were spent enthralled of this tale of healing and reconciliation. I had never read a book like this before. I learned that she had written books as a non-Christian and then found faith which transformed her writing. It would be Francine Rivers who would throw me into studying the Bible like I had never done before. My Bible devotion was brought to life because of this godly author.

Sadie and I enjoyed lots of quiet snuggles while in the NICU. I would sing to her and wrote her a little lullaby, one she still loves when I sing to her. When Bailey asked what his lullaby was, I quickly remembered our favourite tune, *Cotton Fields* by Creedance Clearwater Revival. We used to snuggle as I sang that tune for hours.

Bailey finally had a sibling. I was so thankful that after the wedding I had given Bailey the right to call Shaun Dad; we both knew he secretly had called him Dad on occasion and this fused us together as a real family. Sadie and her big brother were very close and still have a powerful bond to this day.

As for my in-laws, they fell head over heels in love. I don't think hearts can open wider than theirs did. Becoming grandparents completely changed them. Our parents both adored their newest grandchild and were all present when we dedicated both Sadie and Bailey at church. It was a happy time. My mother was finally a grandma without the extra responsibilities. She did have some adjustments to deal with as she and I were used to partnering closely in raising Bailey, but now Shaun was very protective when it came to our family time. My mother and I had to revamp our whole relationship from co-dependency to a more normal grandmother kind of relationship, and it wasn't easy for either of us.

It took Shaun a while to adjust to fatherhood. He did not know what to expect with having a new baby and I will never forget the first time we bundled

Sadie into the car seat and she made that weird facial expression that meant she was going to need a diaper change. "How often does this sort of thing happen?" Shaun asked. I gave him a sad smile as I unbundled our daughter and said, "Forever, honey. This kind of thing will happen for the rest of our lives."

Shaun knew very well how much I had always longed to be a daddy's girl. I had asked him to always be close with his daughters before we had children. Shaun loved his little girl and took his turns in the middle of the night for special bonding times.

Shaun always had a desire to move out west and decided to take a job in Fort McMurray for some new experiences with his trade. I was nervous about him going. For a few weeks after we got home from the hospital, I hadn't felt right. I lacked the confidence to do simple things like taking Sadie for a walk, figuring out what to make for supper, and definitely would never dream of doing things out of my comfort zone. I felt the depression come on strong whenever I would breastfeed and I definitely did not understand then what hormone imbalances I was dealing with. Wanting to be a supportive wife to Shaun, I agreed to the job out west, hoping his inner tug to move to Alberta was a short phase.

I had a hard time juggling all the grandparents. Shaun's mom had become very jealous of my mother and I felt pressures to keep the relationships equal but thought it wasn't fair. I had a strong relationship with my mother but struggled with honour and respect as I felt her control was too much. When I was a young teen mom, we had developed a bond that was too intense for me and I couldn't completely cleave to my husband when I was still co-dependent with my mother. Shaun found this very frustrating as I was not completely submitted to our marriage. My relationship with Shaun's mother was also wavering as I could not deal with her newfound possessive nature. She had not expected to fall head over heels with Sadie but her granddaughter became everything to her. I was thankful that Shaun was in agreement that our parents were both being overbearing. (We were the first to have children on both sides of our family so in many ways this was understandable.) My father we didn't see as regularly as his life in Pinecreek kept him busy but we shared some special times visiting in Pinecreek with our new young family

Life was getting more difficult with Shaun working for twenty-one days straight and then home for only a short while. He was missing Sadie's first year and it was clear we were not doing well without him. He decided to put in his notice at the end of summer and come home. His foreman was from Cold Lake, Alberta, and he offered Shaun a position with Pyramid at Imperial Oil.

Shaun and I discussed the option of moving. We prayed about the decision and discussed our plans with our parents. Feeling guilt-ridden about moving away, we discussed it with our minister. Pastor Dave clearly stated that God doesn't care where you live as long as you are living for Him. Shaun wanted to move with his father's blessing but sadly would not get it. Shaun and I wanted to learn on our own to thrive as a family. There is incredible growth that takes place when you move from home to a new area. You learn to rely on God for all things and know He is there. I trusted my husband and had faith to follow

There were no houses on the market in 2005 in Alberta but Shaun found a rental property that would be suitable—the only problem being that we were eighteenth on the waiting list. Shaun decided to step out in faith and ask the owner of the house if they could meet for coffee. He agreed and Shaun asked him if he had ever considered selling the property. Soon we went from being low on the list to rent to being the new owners.

We moved to Cold Lake on Thanksgiving weekend. Cold Lake is a city that is diverse as any you can imagine due to the oil field and the military base. Getting used to the jets flying through the air was an adjustment but soon became the sound of home. Due to the jobs in the area, Cold Lake was full of young families, to the point that there wasn't even a care home to be seen. Portage had been much more of a retirement town so this was a change for us. It didn't take long for us to find a church that we called home. Shaun had met some co-workers who attended the same church and we became fast friends.

The pain of physical homesickness hit me once again, I remembered all too well this feeling from when I moved as a little girl from Pinecreek. Here I was again, except this time it was my mother that I was cut off from. I believe that this was definitely a divine intervention, leading me to becoming an independent woman. Shaun and I both grieved the loss of close families for we knew moving twelve hours away was not going to be easy. We were all going through the adjustment phase and we did it together. A big blessing was that my little sister lived only three hours away in Edmonton and we were thankful she was close. Bailey was very excited for he loved his Aunty Anna very much.

Stresses were always present and our arguing seemed to increase after the move. Not understanding each other's personality led to many disagreements. I was sensitive and Shaun couldn't figure out why we couldn't just do things his way. His motto was "if you don't like it then leave" or the classic "It's your job"—this, of course, referring to everything in the housewife handbook. Shaun grew up very independently and was used to doing things his way, and you definitely didn't mess with his food. There was no trying different things and he just loved his basic menu. I gave in the majority of the time. This led to living Shaun's way and forgetting about who I was. If something was changed, there would be a rant from my hubby about the need for Basic Shaun Cooking. I chose to just try and make him happy and comply but this would only work for so long.

It was early on in our move that I went up to the front of church and asked for prayer for my anger problem. The pastor was a genuinely kind man and we instantly loved him and his wife. As I stood asking for prayer, my husband came up behind me and admitted that we were both at fault, and there we stood before God and asking for intervention into our stress-filled lives. Thus began our healing journey to find peace and harmony. We would partner with our pastor and his wife for godly mentorship. It was also around this time that our pastor's wife told me about a young military woman who was desperate for childcare and asked me to pray for the need. I thought to myself, "I will pray, but I can definitely tell you I don't want to be the babysitter." As the week went on I just could not leave this thought alone. I was very resistant to the fact that I could babysit—after all, Shaun and I had decided that I would take an extra year off to help us settle and to be there for Bailey as the move was tough on him too. I decided to pray about the babysitting idea. Before I knew what hit me, I was excited to take on the challenge. As I called the pastor's wife to tell her that I thought it was me who was to take this position, she agreed. So it began. I didn't realize God's motive when I accepted the position. That is why it is so crucial that we ask God for direction because He has such huge plans for our lives and sends specific seasons for growth. Here I thought I was doing this family a favour. I quickly embraced the two children and grew to call their mother my friend.

For almost a year I babysat Monday through Friday and what came of this time were the best times of spiritual devotion that I had ever had. Every afternoon while the kids napped, I would routinely do my devotions and I grew tremendously in my faith. I spoke with God and I knew He heard me. Around this time my cousin sent me some Christian literature and challenged me to read it. I read her note: *To Jenny, may this book help you as it has helped me. It has taught me a lot. May you and Shaun grow more together in God. When you honour your husband by being his helper, you honour God. Love, Loretta.*

My first reaction was one of stubborn pride. What was she thinking sending me a book on marriage? What had she heard? Did she think that she had a better marriage than I did? My heart was growing from irritation to anger. All my thoughts were shut down quickly when on the phone she confirmed she herself had been completely annoyed and irritated when her sister Brenda had given *her* the book. Loretta encouraged me to brave through this book and see where the Holy Spirit would discern for me to change. It was a cruel reality, she recalled, when she came upon a piece of truth in the literature that showed her angry bitter heart and she began to change her attitude. I listened in awe of her humility. She encouraged me further by stating that she had received a speech from her husband confirming what a change he had found in their marriage. I was both intrigued and eager to read the book and asked God to help me discern the areas in my marriage where I could find issues. After all, Shaun and I had already learned so much the hard way; this hopefully could be a different approach.

What I was about to find would be more effective then I could have ever imagined. Once again I had some apologizing to do. It was here that I was hit head-on with the truth of what God intended for a marriage and the specific role of the wife, the Proverbs 31 woman. My brain was filled with information that jarred my heart with the truth of my past ignorance. I was stirred by what all the Scriptures had to say about a wife's character and the honour that a husband feels when a wife serves him. *What?* I remember thinking. *My mother had been following in the biblical example of what God asked of every wife?* To make matters even worse, so was also every Hutterite woman that I had ever witnessed. *Great,* I thought, *here was the whole reason that you should get a plate, put some food on it and serve it to your ever-waiting Prince Charming of a husband.* By this time in our marriage, I definitely didn't call Shaun my Prince Charming. I still loved him but most of the time he drove me nuts and I was on many occasions beginning to feel that I didn't like him any more.

As I kept reading I learned about the importance of respecting and honouring your man, and how much it is God's will for every married woman. How could I possibly have been wrong in all my ideals that a man should not be served? I called my mother and told her what I was reading and she just calmly confirmed that, yes, that's where the standard came from. "So, you and every Hutterite woman out there serve the men first because it's what God desires to be proper?" I was as annoyed as ever while I asked her this question, and was even speechless.

As I hung up the phone and stared at the wall, my ignorance began to crumble away, slowly taking with it my bad attitude. My most famous line had always been, "Thank God my parents moved off the Hutterite colony for I would have been the most disrespectful and defiant wife out there." My poor hubby. But the more I read, the more I began to feel conviction and the desire to change this bad attitude that I had harboured for so long. It was exciting for me to finally figure out the beauty of submitting to a husband but I still had a long way to go in learning to trust and love God more than my husband.

It was astonishing to me when I read Proverbs 31 how much Hutterite women mould their lives in this manner. Girls are mentored from a young age and by the time they are married they have a full and biblical understanding on what God expects from a noble Hutterite wife.

I decided that I needed to apologize to the women in my culture. My Aunt Clara is someone that I have often looked up to as a Hutterite woman of noble character. I thought if I apologized to her for disrespecting my heritage then she would stand for all Hutterite women whom I had silently cursed and disrespected. Next was my mother, and in an emotional speech, I told her I was sorry for all the times I was angry at her for serving my father and treating him with honour when I thought he didn't deserve it. I now understood all that I had witnessed of women of noble character honouring their husbands. Making them a plate of food was not sending a message that they were slaves or servants but that they were serving honour by dishing out nourishment.

I had a dilemma in my mission to change: my husband had grown up to be very independent and would never allow me to serve him. He also had mocked the Hutterite culture. To him the men being served looked foolish and he told me that he would not feel comfortable to have a woman serve him. Our upbringings were different; this would definitely be a challenge. I knew that this required discernment from God; this definitely was something I wanted to change in my marriage but I did not want to force my husband to comply by my sudden act of submission during mealtime. So after some prayer and seeking wisdom from above I came up with a plan: I would make Shaun's lunch, I knew that he prided himself with making his own lunch but I really wanted to make it my mission.

It took some getting used to, and in the beginning felt like it was just another thing for me to do. I was committed to my challenge and made a great effort to accomplish the goal. Also I was not and still am not a morning person and my husband would wake up at five a.m. I decided I would just pack his lunch the evening before after everyone had settled. Shaun was annoyed but soon gave in to my new mission. I enjoyed making his lunch and poured as much love and honour into the task as I could. I prayed while I packed his nourishing meal. I left notes and sometimes even cut his sandwich in the shape of a heart. (He expressed his displeasure of this the first time he unpacked his cupid-style sandwich at work—and the boys in the lunch room made much fun of the love sandwich. He liked to remind me often, "Please don't cut my sandwich with that stupid heart-shaped thing!" I only did it a few more after that, hiding his sandwich in a disguised manner so that he wouldn't notice the shape until he got to work.) It was a task that I soon looked forward to and my creativity was proving the possibilities were endless.

After a while my husband told me that he needed me to know how much confidence he had as a man because I made his lunch every day, that when work was tough and life was bleak, it was the simple things I did that made all the difference. My cousin had told me that I would be getting a speech from my husband if I truly implemented something to change my character, but I never expected a speech like this one. Shaun commented many times that he felt the love and honour from just me making his lunch, my serving him a meal. This all made sense now and I saw for myself why every Hutterite woman had dished out the men's meals. It had nothing to do with being a lesser class but it simply was the fact that it was an honour to serve another. After all didn't Jesus Himself come to serve and not be served? He even washed His disciples' feet just to prove this very point.

Needless to say our marriage was changed and my husband said it best when one day he said that our marriage reached a new level when I learned to serve and he learned to be served. It is amazing how vulnerable a man is when a woman treats him with honour. I have made my husband's plate many times since then and enjoy the honour it brings him. I even find it romantic for he gets to feel like a king at our very own dining room table. My mother has teased him often that he now allows this biblical form of respect.

Another cherished memory from this time occurred when my husband was lamenting about a co-worker and his complaints about his marriage. As Shaun was trying to explain the dilemma in their marriage, he just said sadly, "Oh, you can definitely tell that his wife doesn't make his lunch!" I laughed but would never judge another woman for I know just how hard a marriage could be. I was just so thankful honour had found its way into mine.

My relationship with Shaun's mother significantly improved with our frequent visits. I loved that she had always been such a good listener and understood my trials of depression and relocation. She and I had an amazing healing in our relationship after I prayed to God and asked Him to show me what He saw when He looked at my mother-in-law. I was overwhelmed with a truth I had never seen before, that she did have an honouring heart and had sacrificed much to move to her husband's home province. I told her that our new names would be Ruth and Naomi, after the biblical story of a mother-in-law whose daughter-in-law had become a widow and legally could return home to her family but instead decided to honour her mother-in-law's faith and remain beside her. I knew that no matter what my mother-in-law had remained beside me in all my struggles and vowed that I would work at cherishing our relationship. We had some very truthful conversations and dealt with a lot of things from the past. I was stunned to realize that she loved me very much and saw me as her own daughter when all this time I had convinced myself that she only tolerated me. The truth that communication brings sheds light on the darkness of our thought patterns and how we perceive things.

Our church was the type that as soon as you walked through the front door you were hit with the anointing of love. You knew these people were real. Worship was vibrant and our spirits soared. Our church was filling up quickly with young families and we knew this definitely was not a town like the ones we were used to. At one of the ladies evening events, I met my cherished friend Danielle. She taught me many things about being a genuine mother and if there was ever a crown given for the authentic mother of the year, then she would wear it rightly. Where my ideas of parenting were tightly reined, hers were about going with the flow. She had grace and confidence and the moment you walked in the door of her home you knew you were welcome.

Our pastor's wife approached me and asked me if I would consider being a camp nurse. I was instantly thrilled as once again this opportunity came my way through a church. Bailey, Sadie and I readied ourselves for a fun-filled few weeks. Camp turned out to be a blast and it was there that I would meet my spiritual mentor. Our minister's wife also told me that her daughter would be at camp for the summer. Cindy and I became instant best friends and still have a very close bond. Little did Shaun and I know that she and her husband would soon become the new senior pastors at Cold Lake Community Church.

15 HEALING AND RECONCILIATION

AS OUR CHURCH GREW, THERE WERE LOTS OF OPPORTUNITIES FOR WORKSHOPS TO help equip young families for success in all their relationships. I attended one of these workshops for the ladies in our church. It was on anger and the facilitator gave us tools to recognize triggers and the cycle of anger. I easily took in this information and learned new ways to break the anger cycle. We learned to look back into our childhood and look for things to be grateful for.

We were asked to take on a challenge and write a letter to both of our parents in honour, to tell them what you would want to say at their funeral. This project sent me to a place of truth. I had been placed between my parents in their ongoing dispute and separation. They had looked at me as their middle-man so often that I had lost my identity as their daughter. I wrote my letters to both my parents, asking their forgiveness and taking my place as their daughter. I would take the long road back to becoming an honourable daughter. Both letters were received by my parents and I shared a heart-to-heart with both. Before I moved to Alberta, my father had asked me to meet him for coffee; when I did he told me of the sermon he had heard not long before. He then took the time to apologize for everything he had ever neglected to give me as a father. He told me he loved me and he was proud of me. With tears in both our eyes, I told him I accepted his apology and forgave him. This letter was my opportunity to thank him for all he had ever done and offering him the honour that he so rightly deserved. My father's reply was light-hearted but I knew my words had reached his heart. My mother's reply was simply that I should not be too hard on myself, that as a young child I had been surrounded with lots of training ground for disrespect and anger.

Acknowledging that this might very well have been the case, I now wanted more than ever to learn to be respectful.

There is blessing attached to honouring your parents and I knew placing myself back in the position of being a daughter was the best step. I would honour and respect my parents and pray for them instead of giving them my opinions on forgiveness. I still made sure to tell my mother that I had placed a picture of her and Dad in happier times on my treadmill and that I was praying hard for my parents to be reconciled. My mothers had a 'it's never going to happen' attitude but I knew inside there had to be a way. I quickly reminded my mother that when I spent time with Jesus, I always got what I wanted. It made me think of my favourite movie, *The Parent Trap*.

There was clearly a shift in our family as I had begun to feel freedom. My sister had moved to Cold Lake, and together we began to pray for our parents. My mother had begun to believe that my father was not to blame for his anger outburst and that he truly did suffer from a manic illness, or bipolar. I hate labels and diagnoses but we couldn't argue that things had gone terribly wrong in my father's life due to an illness. I was beginning to put more and more things together, between what I had learned in college and what I was learning through Bible teachings and seminars. The type of illness that my father suffered from had definitely started with a trauma.

It became evident that God had placed Cindy Steeves into my life as my spiritual mentor. It was as if she was the mediator between me and God as she continuously reinforced God's love for me and she showered me with words of affirmation. Never in my life had I had this kind of friend. She was very instrumental in steering my prayers in the right direction and taught me much about God's character when it came to forgiveness and she showed me biblical examples of what unconditional love was and what damage a condemning attitude could bring. I had never realized how judgmental of a person I had really become. The Scriptures she showed me (Ephesians 6:12) proved that we do not wage war against flesh and bone but against spirits and principalities. She taught me that we are to love each person where they are at. Love is a choice!

During one of my devotions and prayer time I received a shocking revelation. I was earnestly searching for truth when I realized what my father's trigger had been in 2001. I could see how he could put up walls around his heart after Glen's death. The small bout of post-partum depression that I had after Sadie was born was enough for me to see how a parent could put up protective walls from their children. I had battled with the thoughts that I was unworthy of these children and that they deserved a better mother. I had begun breaking off this condemning threat, remembering that God had chosen me as their mother, and through my relationship with Jesus, I would find all I needed to raise them. But I could see why my father would push us away, especially after my brother's death. Dad put up the walls so that he couldn't hurt us and we couldn't reach that beautiful place in his heart he now kept vaulted.

My father's triggers after my brother's death had been every Christmas and, of course, every Thanksgiving. Then, when Bailey was born and my father held him the first time, saying in a quiet voice, "He looks like Johnny Boy"—the next day my father had a mental breakdown. His next episode had happened in 2001, which was the year Bailey turned six, the same age Glen had been when he died. I couldn't believe the connection and told my mother of my theory.

Shaun and I were expecting our third child and I began to feel a huge longing to name this baby after my brother if it was a boy. I asked my husband his blessing and, after he gave it some thought, he agreed. I thought my mother would probably think this was a crazy idea. I feared her reaction and thought she might even be angered by my idea. I had a very strong reassurance that this was the right thing to do but was not ready for my mother's response. On the phone, I asked for my mother's blessing to name this child after my brother if the baby was to be a boy. My mother was quiet on the phone and then in a voice that was cracking with emotion, she responded, "It would be so nice to be able to say that name again." I sat stunned. I was not expecting this reaction. Mom explained that she had not spoken that name in years for my father had forbidden it. I remembered now for the first time that this had indeed been the cruel reality for us as a family. We decided that we would wait to tell my father.

My father was living an unpredictable life, with lots of irrational behaviour. It was heart-wrenching to think of my dad all alone in the world, and to hear the many calls from family members informing us of his latest episodes. I tried to stay in touch with Dad but often found my emotions erupting with fear and pain. My sister and I continued to pray with our mother over these situations, even fasting and praying. We desperately wanted a stable life for our father. He had been living on his own again and that extra stress seemed to take its toll on Dad's life. My mother had a Christian friend say that she could see how much pride my mother had and that Mom was resisting forgiving my father. My mother confessed to me that she was furious at this comment for the woman saw right through her. I had no idea that this began the mission in my mother's life to begin the process of forgiveness. (My mother would later say that she feared forgiving my father and that it took five years to unravel the pain and pride before God put a song in heart written by the Holy Spirit that showed her the path to freedom.)

While my pregnancy was continuing, my friend Cindy and I had proclaimed healing and reconciliation over my parents and we prayed this prayer feverishly.

During one of my conversations with my father, I discovered a truth. Although his irrational behaviour was unstable, there was always a small degree of truth in what he was saying. Everyone had stopped believing and listening to my father, which for the most part was understandable, but I began to realize that he was being misunderstood the majority of the time. So I began to listen carefully to my father and this new idea proved wise. My father told me he had began to listen to Joyce Meyers and really enjoyed her straight-to-the-point preaching, and we began to have many conversations about those messages. Our conversations were more stable and our relationship was growing even stronger. We never missed an opportunity to pray for Mom; we prayed that they would get back together and that our family would be whole again. I will forever cherish those days praying with my dad

One day, I received a phone call from my father, and he seemed both calm and anxious. He told me in a soft voice that he had had a dream and that God had spoken to him. My new vow to always listen with an open mind was useful. My father told me that God said he was going to go into a dark valley and that he would not be alone for Jesus would always be with him but that he should remain strong. After he made it throught the valley, God promised my father a new bride. My dad became excited about this and said, "Jenny, then I saw you held Mom's hand and brought her to me." My heart skipped a beat and I quickly had both panic and excitement running through my veins. I truly believed my father but feared that my father would now take this literally and think I was to get Mom and take her by the hand to my father. My father proved to me that this dream from heaven was more than enough to fill his heart and soul and he seemed to have a newfound peace. Of course, he told everyone who would listen about his dream from heaven. Sadly, most people still thought he was unstable. I believed my father had definitely heard from God but didn't understand how it would all turn out. After all hadn't my father already been through enough dark valleys and now according to the dream he was to go through his darkest one yet.

My pregnancy was coming along well and I still enjoyed working part time at the hospital and taking care of our busy home. I loved being pregnant and was always the happiest during my pregnancies. It was after childbirth that everything always became difficult for me. I was looking forward to my early November baby and was pretty certain it was to be a boy. I was excited to name him Glen.

My little man had other plans, arriving on October 3—eight weeks early and having to be taken by air ambulance from Cold Lake to Edmonton. At just over five pounds, he proved he was to be a determined child. We named him Glen Lawrence Rumancik, after my little brother and Shaun's dad, Lawrence (Larry), our treasured Papa. He was quickly nicknamed Handsome Little Man by his dad. We were all in a whirlwind. Bailey and Sadie loved their little brother and couldn't get enough. My father flew in to meet his grandson and with tears he held his little grandson as I got to tell my father that his name was Glen. There was an amazing presence of peace in the room and I was so thankful that my father was there. I knew that it was indeed the right decision to name my son Glen for the healing and reconciliation had begun. We celebrated Glen's birth and were so thankful that he was born healthy, although early. My parents finally had a reason to say the name Glen once again—I was sure Uncle Glen in heaven was very proud.

Bailey and Sadie loved their little brother's courageous little spirit and we bought Glen a stuffed tiger to prove just what a brave little man he was. We had some good times as a family making videos for my mother of Glen sunbathing in the incubator. He held his hands up over his head with his little eye coverings in place, looking like he was enjoying a day at the beach. I was so thankful for the quiet time that the NICU gave us and I feel it was God's way of ensuring I got some much needed peace and quiet before coming home to our busy household. I was thankful that Shaun's mother was there to help Shaun with the crew at home. My mother would also be arriving soon and I couldn't wait for her to meet Glen. I also couldn't wait to see how Mom would look as she had been working on a new healthy lifestyle and had lost a lot of weight. My family members back home had all commented how young and healthy she looked. She had also just been nominated as "queen" by her TOPS (Taking Pounds Off Sensibly) weight loss group, a group that was very supportive and which is still very dear to her. Mom's younger brother, our Uncle Andy, joked with Mom and called her the queen.

When Mom arrived and was introduced to her new grandson, her tears confirmed that her pain was still as real as it had been twenty-three years before. She said his name in a soft whisper and enjoyed the warmth that filled her heart. As freedom began to flow through her heart, the walls came crumbling down. We enjoyed her visit and I so appreciated that she was there. Mom definitely looked amazing and we all confirmed that she did look like royalty.

One day after Mom had gone back home and I had left some money on the table, Sadie climbed up and looked at the twenty-dollar bill, asking why Grandma was on the money. The only difference Sadie noticed was that the queen had very pronounced lips. Uncle Andy had great fun with this new information that Sadie had newly anointed her grandma as the queen. I couldn't argue the fact that my mother looked just as elegant as the Queen of England. Mom was shocked by her granddaughter's comment but had to receive the kind words.

Once Glen and I were home, it didn't take long for life to get busy and for post-partum depression to set in again. I hung on to my faith and tried my best to get through it, but I struggled with anger and anxiety. I just didn't feel right and knew it wasn't your typical baby blues. I did not know then that having a preemie put you at higher risk for having issues with this hormonally imbalanced state. Shaun did not understand the mixture of anxiety and depression I felt. My husband was having his own issues with dealing with work, life and a growing family. Always concerned with our financial well being, he definitely felt the stresses this brought. I was definitely thankful for the growth I had had as a wife to be more supportive of my husband and to remember to make him a priority too.

I decided to go back to work early and just work part-time as this would be a good way for me to balance my sanity. I enjoyed my job as an LPN and really enjoyed my co-workers. My co-worker Jen became a very special friend and we had much in common. I loved our friendship and felt our relationship helped when it came to balancing both home and work. Jen also had a young child, so we became fitness partners.

I was thankful for our congregation and for my friends who had young families also. My closest friends Danielle and Cindy both were pregnant at the same time as I was so they were a big support. The only problem was that whenever we would try to get together, we would have an army of kids around us but we did it anyways and we made many memories. Shaun and I finally felt like we were getting a grip on this marriage thing and although we had a long way to go we were becoming a happy, strong family—aside from my emotional outbursts.

My friend Cindy asked if I would come to an In the Gap prayer evening that would pray for my family's situation. This evening would prove to be greater than I could ever imagine. Intercessors are those who have the spiritual gift to hear from the Lord easily. On an evening in mid-May, I arrived at church, eager to participate in any healing event that church could bring my way.

Pastor Lance and his wife Cindy explained the importance of this type of prayer, and laid out the instructions for this kind of spiritual encounter with God. It was then I was asked to come to the front of the church and give an account of my life from birth to age seventeen. When I was finished, I was drained by the emotions and all that my life had entailed. Soon the floor was open to prayer and anything that the people who prayed for me felt. What came out of them was amazing truth, things I had not spoken but also things that I had already walked through with God, my father and my mother. It was a confirmation that I was on the right track in my faith walk with Jesus as the centre of my life. Pastor Lance spoke and with a voice of authority he proclaimed that the walls that my father had placed up would come down and that there would be a flood of healing love to surround my dad.

After my evening at church I was excited about my family's future but didn't expect instant results. Our family had a long way to go, or so I thought. I was not expecting the phone call that came from my father just one week after the prayer event. I was used to the phone calls that would come from my parents where one of them would say "Have you talked to your father today?" or "Have you talked to your mother today?" I really found this annoying but usually did my part in giving them the appropriate response. This time, though, I was at a loss for what to say. My father told me that my mother had actually walked up to him and had a conversation with him. He had been sitting on a bench in front of a coffee shop reading a paper when he noticed Mom's car parking across the street. He said she sat in the car a while and then got out and began to cross the street. He was speaking in a very peculiar tone as if he was still trying to figure out what had just happened. I listened with complete disbelief; I couldn't believe what he was telling me. Mom had not willingly spoken to my father in eight years, not even at my wedding. He said that my mother walked right up to him. Standing in front of him she quietly said "Hi. How are you?" She asked if he had had supper and if he needed any money or if she could make him supper. That my father didn't erupt in anger at her question was a miracle as this usually would have sent Dad into a prideful rage. My dad simply stated that he said he was fine and then proceeded to lie, saying that he had already had supper. He said he wasn't going to push it and have supper with Mom for his heart was full. Remembering Pastor Lance's words just one week prior, I felt that this was unreal. My mother's phone call came later in the day. "Have you heard from your father today?" I thought about lying but didn't. She confirmed Dad's story just as he had stated. She said that she just felt a need to speak to him and took the first opportunity. I phoned Shaun and eagerly shared with him the news, and then called Pastor Lance and notified the prayer group. My siblings and I celebrated this news. We had been through a lot of family turmoil and family interventions. This seemed to to give us new hope.

My father's health had begun to decline and he had been known in our local hospital as a frequent flyer. Because of his emotional struggles he definitely was falling through the cracks of the medical system. I received a phone call from my mother one evening that my father had been seen sitting in the emergency department of the local hospital. Being far away in Alberta, I felt helpless but this time was the worst. The caller had told my mother that my father looked horrible. I called the hospital and they told me that my father was going to be admitted to the medical ward. The next day when I called to see what Dad's condition was, I was stunned to hear that my father had never been admitted to the medical ward but was instead in the Intensive Care Unit. I frantically phoned my mother and couldn't talk through the fear and sobs. I felt helpless. My mother said words that I will never forget. "I will go to the hospital and see your father on behalf of you kids." Thankful and hopeful, I waited for her reply. When Mom arrived at the hospital, they told her my father was dealing with a bad septic infection and was in serious condition. My father had been complaining of a sore leg for weeks but no one had given him the proper medical attention which now led to his serious condition. My mother later told me that when my father opened his eyes momentarily and saw her, he quietly said, "None of it was your fault. I'm sorry." He tried to say more but Mom told him to rest and that it was okay. I wept when my mother informed me and she told me that she would be there to check on Dad; she had finally found forgiveness.

My father was rushed to Winnipeg as his condition continued to worsen and his body began to shut down, and on Father's Day we all surrounded his bedside, even his precious Anna. She held his hand and he squeezed back. He began to finally be able to breathe again thanks to swift medical intervention. We knew that it was also heavenly intervention. Sadie climbed onto her Papa's bed and sweetly said, "It's okay, Papa. I'm here now." We all laughed at the certainty with which she spoke. When Dad looked around the room, he saw every one of us standing there, his children and their significant others, and my mother. He didn't like it when he could not see her and showed great signs of stress whenever she left his bedside. Who could blame him as he had waited seven long years for this. They had not reconciled but at least she was there.

As Dad began to recover, he was sent home to our local hospital. During his recovery Dad began to act peculiar and, due to a lack of communication between medical staff, great neglect was made regarding Dad's care. The staff feared Dad was having a psychiatric breakdown and got doctor's orders to send him back to Winnipeg for a psychiatric assessment. Dad's brothers were shocked at how my father was being mistreated and we were stunned to find out that in order to be properly assessed by a psychiatrist my father would have to go by police escort. How disgusted we were with the health system when they failed to take into consideration that my father had been on life support just one week prior. My uncles begged to take him in their own vehicles. They would not allow any other means of transportation. The only measure of peace we had was that our Uncle Steve requested that our Aunty Sara ride with my dad in the cruiser, and that this was allowed.

My father was placed into a police cruiser and transported back to Winnipeg for a psychiatric assessment. Shaun and I along with my Uncle Steve and Aunt Sara spent our wedding anniversary at Dad's side in the emergency department waiting for a psychiatrist. All the while there were two police officers from Portage standing guard at Dad's bedside. They had orders to remain with the patient until an evaluation was complete.

This seemed so stupid and cruel to all involved but I truthfully declare that I would do it all over again. I know now that sometimes God allows all these things for his greater purpose. For God had a great plan and we were all about to witness Dad's heavenly dream come to pass, the one about the dark valley and the promise of a new bride.

In the middle of the night, a psychiatrist came and did his evaluation and by morning he informed us all that my father showed absolutely no signs of bipolar or manic illness but clearly was suffering from a case of delirium, initially caused by his many days in the ICU.

The RCMP officers each in turn apologized to my father on behalf of the police force for the great neglect he had faced in the last day. As they shook his hand, they said something I hope to never forget, "Mr. Maendel, you are a true gentleman." I saw the look on my father's face and I knew what that meant to him.

The doctor then informed us that my father was to be discharged back to our local hospital and we were devastated; none of us wanted my father there again. I had been keeping my mother updated and called her again with raw emotions. I just wanted to pack Dad up and take him back to Alberta. He was very weak and could not go home alone to his quiet little country home. My mother cut me off as my tears were pouring out, "You can tell your dad that it's time to come home." I was stunned and she repeated herself. I gave a shout, rushed over and told my aunt who grabbed the phone and spoke to her sister just to hear it for herself. We were all speechless. My father was sitting on the side of his bed and I walked up to my dad and placed my forehead on his and said, "Hey Dad, guess where you're going?" I then told him that Mom had said it was time to come home. I hugged my dad and we both knew that our prayers had finally been answered. We had been praying for years. My Aunty Sara told all the immediate family of the good news. Everyone had been praying for my parents to reconcile for so long. As I turned to inform the doctor of our decision, I shook his hand and thanked him for closing the doors on the possibility that my father could have been admitted and informed him that the right door was now opened that my father was finally going to be reconciled with Mom.

While I was speaking with the doctor, my Uncle Steve hollered for me to come and see. I looked and there was my father jigging and singing that this was his Holy Spirit jig and that he was finally going home. We all stood as his honoured audience. Praise to the Lord God. This all made sense to us now: the RCMP escort, the need for a psychiatric evaluation, the denial by all physicians to admit my father onto any floor of Winnipeg hospital for further recovery. He was going to the only place that God had intended, home with Mom! My father's dream of God's promise had been fulfilled and, just five weeks after the prayer meeting, Shaun and I drove Dad to Mom's, the day before their wedding anniversary. Just like he said, "And you will bring your Mom to me, Jenny." I felt like I had truly become a faithful daughter, standing by my mother through prayer and support as she forgave Dad. I guess in God's way I had led her to Dad because I had never given up on reconciliation. It was my spiritual version of *The Parent Trap.* As for the new bride part, my mother looked stunning and with forgiveness now in her heart, she was radiant, glowing in the beauty that only Christ alone could grant. Dad indeed had a new bride! I love the fact that my father told so many people of his encounter with God and now they all stood as witnesses to God's faithfulness.

The next day, on their wedding anniversary, Mom and Dad were blessed with a new grandchild and Shaun and I went to meet my brother Conrad and his girlfriend, Rose, who had had their first child, Conner. I was so thankful that my brother got such a gift to have both Mom and Dad arrive together to meet his son. Conrad had been there as a very close support when things got most difficult with Dad. We both wanted a healthy relationship with our father and we finally had one.

I recalled a few years before when I had been pouring out my heart to my brother about my dissatisfaction of love in our family. I was lamenting to the fact that he and I were not close anymore and I challenged him that maybe he had never even cared about his big sister. He stunned me with his next comment. "You tell me of any other girl you know that had squirrel-skinned Barbie rugs in her Barbie house when they were twelve years old!" It took me a moment but then I remembered waking up and finding this small dried carcass on the top floor of my little Barbie mansion. My brother described how he had shot the squirrel, skinned it and dried it out in the sun with his homemade frame made from small but sturdy sticks, before stealing more of Mom's perfume to make sure it smelled good. Yes, indeed my brother did love me—not many girls can say they received a squirrel-skin Barbie rug from their brothers—and this little brother of mine deserved this blessing of having the first picture of both Mom and Dad reconciled at the celebration of the birth of his son.

We also made a stop at Uncle Steve and Aunt Sara's for the reconciliation tour. As we sat outside in the warm June sun we were soon joined by my grandmother Rachel who had been the first person Aunty Sara had called to inform that her son had reconciled with his wife and that he was finally home. It was an anointed visit and one that I am thankful to have been a part of. Some more relatives arrived and it was a reunion like none of us had ever known.

***

Shaun and I decided to complete our family with child number four and we were expecting her arrival in early spring. Our family we felt would be complete and we were all excited for her arrival.

Bailey was doing better in school after he had begun taking medication to help him focus. Shaun and I noticed an improvement in his behaviour at home. He had always been an easygoing kid, very compliant and happy; he just didn't seem to have the same social cues that kids his age had which led to him having many difficulties with social skills. We enjoyed many outings as a family exploring the northern lakes surrounding Cold Lake. We had many fun-filled memories where our dogs, Charlie Brown and King, would enjoy some competitive swims trying to catch the biggest stick.

Glen was just nine months old when my parents reconciled. He was growing so fast in spirit and size, and he and his big sister Sadie were very close. She reminded me of myself when I was a little sister and proved she was just as over-protective as I had been. Glen was short and pudgy and had a very round face and no hair so he caught people's attention. I loved chewing on his big round cheeks and began telling him at a very young age that he had helped Grandma and Papa to fall in love again, that his kisses were medicine and his hugs were bandaids. Glen was a perfect combination of rough and tender, and always kept us on our toes. His big brother would just watch his antics in awe and wonder.

Then, in mid-August while I was working an evening shift at the hospital, I got the horrible call that my father had had a heart attack. Dad had collapsed right in front of my mother in their living room. We were all devastated and we rushed to Dad's side once again, driving all night to see him. Tests quickly revealed that my father would need surgery to repair some valves in his heart. My parents were taking all precautions necessary to ready my father for surgery but it would not be an easy fix. My father recovered in hospital and then was sent home to prepare for surgery hopefully in the next few months. We were all shaken and could not bear the thought of losing Dad after all we had been through. It was clear that my father had done serious damage to his heart and lungs with years of over-stressed situations. We hoped that this new surgery would give my father many more years to come.

Dad was enjoying his time with Mom but she could tell how full of fear he was and that he really didn't want to go through with the surgery. He also feared death. There were many phone calls where he pleaded with me for Shaun and me to move home. Sadie and Glen were growing to love their grandfather and Sadie often phoned her papa to sing to him. Their favourite song was *I Have Decided to Follow Jesus*, and my father and Sadie would sing this tune over the phone many times. It touched my heart at how certain Sadie was about just what her Papa needed. My father was rather lonely now that this cardiac prognosis had left him simply resting at home for the majority of the time, so phone calls from his grandchildren were a treasured time. My brother Conrad and his young family had also bonded with Dad and their son Conner always recognized his Papa immediately upon entering the room.

We were so looking forward to the Christmas season as this would be the first family Christmas since the year 2001. My sister Anna was planning to arrive a few days prior to the holidays so that she could spend some quality time with Mom and Dad alone. My sister's relationship with our dad was proof of how much had been accomplished by the power of Jesus and the blood He shed on the cross. My father was really looking forward to her visit and he spoke with enthusiasm as we shared a fun-loving chat on the phone one afternoon. My mother was working that afternoon and I was teasing my father about what he would get my mom for a Christmas present. I spoke with complete joy running through my heart, "Hey Dad, are you gonna pop the question to Mom this Christmas?" My father quickly replied "Oh no! That would be too scary!" My father and I often talked about the healing and reconciliation of their love and that, even though they had completely divorced in the court's eyes, they believed that in Christ they were married with a new and anointed marriage vow.

I wasn't the only one who enjoyed the teasing moments with Dad. A few days before my sister was to arrive, my brothers Conrad and Elias stopped in at Mom and Dad's early in the evening. Mom offered to cook up a frozen pizza for the boys and they quickly accepted her offer. The boys asked where Dad was, and Mom had then commented that Dad had been going to bed earlier lately and was more fatigued in the evenings. The boys then tiptoed into the bedroom and found Dad fast asleep. Dad woke in a pleasant state to find both his sons encouraging him to join them for a late-night snack. My mother said they had a great time and Dad was so happy to see them.

Our lives were all shattered when on December 17 my mother came home to find that my father had suffered a massive cardiac arrest. She knew that hope of reviving Dad was all but impossible. She called my brother Elias since he lived the closest, and he was soon at my mother's side. Paramedics tried to revive my father but there were no signs of hope. When I received the call in Alberta twelve hours away, I gave a gut-wrenching scream. My husband wrapped his arms around me as I wept in disbelief and shock. He was supposed to have surgery and then we would have years of family memories to live out. The call for Dad's surgery would come a few weeks after his funeral, tragically too late. This was not possible! Not fair! We were just a week shy of our first family Christmas; it had only been six months since our parents had reconciled. This was a tragedy that none of us wanted to believe. My mother recalled pounding her fists against the walls and screaming out that it was not fair, that they hadn't had long enough, that it was all too small of a glimpse of what their marriage could be.

So the plans were made a few days before Christmas to lay my father to rest. I became furious with my mother when she refused to have my father's funeral in our large family church but she stood her ground that she would not allow my father to be dishonoured by people who claimed to know Christ but couldn't even understand my mother's decision to forgive and reconcile with my father. I was horrified to learn that many people that I had looked up to in the Christian church had all but failed to see the beauty of true forgiveness. So it was to be that my father's funeral was a small intimate gathering at one of our funeral homes in our local town. As we all stood around my father's casket to say our final goodbyes we all sang our Dad's cherished song, *I Have Decided to Follow Jesus.* Yes, my father had lived his life to follow Jesus and never once to my knowledge did he ever turn his back on his faith.

Once again my uncles worked together to reunite our family with the traditions of our heritage. My Uncle Lorenze made the final declaration that my father would receive a Hutterite burial as honouring as one could get. The funeral was large and many Hutterite ministers spoke well of my father and shook my mother's hand in recognition of my father's life. They also made it well known that he deserved to be honoured and my mother had not one financial obligation to the cost of Dad's funeral. Many Hutterite members of the church agreed that it was an honour to pay for the cost. As my sister stood in the dining hall in our cherished Pinecreek colony, she spoke clearly of the overwhelming care we accepted from all involved. She thanked every Hutterite present for all they had done for our family. It was well spoken and well received. My father would have been very proud of his little Anna. As we all sat surrounding my father's casket in the living room of my grandparents' home we sang the old popular hymns. The house was filled and we all felt the presence of the Lord. It was here that we all witnessed the bravery of one little girl. In front of a room full of Hutterite members, this little four-year-old girl requested they sing her Papa's favourite song, *I Have Decided to Follow Jesus.* My daughter Sadie spoke with such determination as all the people in the room looked at her with awe of her bravery. We sang for her the cherished song.

Then my father was carried by the chosen pallbearers all the way to the cemetery, a final picture of the greatest honour one could receive at a Hutterite funeral. In the big picture, we all knew that my father's life had come full circle as he was home fully reconciled and buried beside his son. We could all just imagine the reunion that happened in heaven when my father finally embraced his little Johnny Boy again. I fully believe that the ones who believe in the Lord Jesus will be reunited immediately in spirit, just like the Scriptures tell of the words of Jesus himself to the sinner on the cross next to him. I believe that my father had my brother wrapped in his arms as soon as he took his last breath.

We tried our best to get through the holiday season. With my father buried just a few days before Christmas, our loss was definitely weighing heavily on all of us. We still could sense the incredible peace and blessing for we as a family were made whole before our father's death. We were so thankful that we had the opportunity to share the love and harmony with Dad in his final few days. We shared our thoughts with Mom and she shared hers. I asked my mother if she ever told Dad she loved him and she confirmed that they had a miracle marriage in their last six months. It was then that I shared my last conversation I had with Dad. My mother confirmed that they both had achieved the greatest honour and respect for one another. We as a family had definitely experienced God's reward for true forgiveness and reconciliation. There were other relatives who also called my mother and told her conversations that Dad had with them privately about Mom, his love for her, her beauty, her character. It all came pouring out to Mom as if she was receiving an unscripted love letter sent from Dad up in heaven. He didn't need anyone to write this one for he had an audience rehearsed and ready to verbalize it to Mom. My mother's heart was full as she received my father's affirmations wholeheartedly. We could all testify as a family that my father had made all things right in his life and we were brave enough to distance ourselves from all those who were still ignorant enought to still speak ill of my father and not understand God's redemptive power.

Once we were back home we were embraced by our congregation and it was confirmed over and over again that my father had definitely died before his time. I still thought it was still so unreal and cruel that my father was gone. The only way I knew how to grieve was to say his name over and over again. Softly I would say those beautiful words, *Dad......Dad......Dad.* It was excruciatingly painful to know that I would never hear his voice again or hold his strong rough hands. We had grown so close at last, and I definitely didn't want to let go of my relationship with him. I even wished death would come to me too so that I could be in heaven too. When I shared this with my husband, he very quickly jolted me back to reality with the response that what I desired was completely selfish and cruel for our young family. Of course he was right and I soon let go of my foolish desire.

One evening while I lay awake in bed, I decided to petition the only One who would understand the debt of my pain, Jesus, my friend, my redeemer. I began to pray desperately to see my father again. I begged and pleaded and asked Jesus to grant me this desperate plea. What I am about to share with you is true. One night in a dream, I saw a beautiful country road. It was a perfect fall day and the sun was a warm yellow amber colour. As I looked down the path I saw someone coming towards me and I soon recognized this man to be my father. I quickly screamed his name. He confirmed it was him as he said my name with out stretched arms. I ran to greet him. He had no hint of uncertainty in his voice and it seemed as if he was not surprised to see me on this country road. I felt the warmth and strength in his fatherly embrace and hung on to him as long as time would allow. I cried large tears and sobbed the words that I missed him as he now heard me say his name over and over again. He spoke with both eagerness and confidence as he lifted my head off his shoulders. "Come, Jenny, I want to show you something!" He then led me to a large brown cabinet that was nearby, one I had not noticed before. When my father opened both doors, I noticed that it was a fridge. He then looked at me and with peace and certainty in his voice, he said "You have no idea how good it feels not to be hungry anymore!" My father was smiling and looked so at peace that I stood speechless. When I awoke that very next morning it didn't take any time to recall the events from my dream. I was stunned at how much this confirmed my father's life. In our family, gluttony was something we struggled with and it was something my father and I also had in common. There were times where we fought for the last pork chop! It was definitely a truthful picture that my father had finally found complete peace with the one thing he still couldn't give up here on earth. My father would definitely not be hungry anymore in the presence of Almighty God. It clearly states in Scripture that he is the bread of life and the salt of the earth. I was at peace after my dream, my gift from above, and I knew that my dad deserved this heavenly rest and I could now let go.

The year 2009 seemed to have the promise that life was only getting better. Shaun and I had been married almost six years and were continuing to grow in love. Our church had continued to multiply and had now almost tripled in the few years we had been attending. There were always opportunities to take in seminars to grow in your faith and workshops to enrich your family life. Our church's mission statement 'Where Families Come Together' was both a literal and spiritual statement.

In March 2009. Shaun and I had the opportunity along with Bailey to take in a new and unique seminar that took a look at your heritage, where you came from. After the seminar there was an opportunity to receive a blessing and individual prayers. As I was at the front of the church I was approached by the facilitator who prayed for me and then felt she had a word for me from God. I was all ears and I loved any spiritual insight I could get. She looked into my eyes and seemed to see right into my heart. What she said next was to become the greatest compliment I had ever received. She spoke with such certainty and her voice was full of awe and wonder. "You have the anointing of Queen Esther!" She then continued with her confirmation by telling me that I had an aura of purple around me, and she encouraged me to study the character of Esther in the Bible. She continued on and told me she could hear my prayers for my son as I petitioned heaven on his behalf. Bailey was standing not too far from us and she asked me quietly if that was my son. I confirmed that he was and this soft-spoken woman proceeded to tell me that he would be an answer to prayer. I loved hearing her words for I had spent many hours petitioning heaven on my son's behalf. I had heard her testimony during the conference and knew she was a mother who also interceded for her child a lot. I fully trusted all she had to tell me. When she was done with her blessing for me, another woman approached me and said confidently to me as she held both my hands, "You are going to go through a season soon where you are going to have to rest in the Lord." I liked the way she spoke in a soft peaceful manner and I concluded that, since I was pregnant, that meant that I would be able to be at home and stay cozy and also be exempt from teaching Sunday school and having to work in the church nursery during Sunday morning services.

Let me inform you now: that is *not* what that was meant. Resting in the Lord basically means: hang on for dear life and do not let go of Jesus for your life is going to get really messy, hard, tearful, strained. All of these words would sum up me having to rest in the Lord in my near future. I tucked that little warning away but asked God to show me all he could about this anointing of Queen Esther, for that was something I wanted to know much about. As Shaun, Bailey, and I left the conference we talked eagerly about our experience, and Shaun said he felt such cleansing peace that he needed no extra blessing; he was truly enlightened. Bailey had been encouraged to let his true personality out and to not hide behind a mask. He was told that he had a warrior spirit and that God was working on his character. He should work hard at just being himself.

The next Sunday morning would come, my friend Cindy, now church women's ministry leader, showed us all a promotional video on what our next Wednesday morning Bible study would be—Esther by Beth Moore. (If you have never heard of Beth Moore let me tell you that she leaves no stone unturned when dissecting a book in the Bible or a Bible character. She is a theologian I have grown to love and cherish. I couldn't wait for the sessions to start and find answers to all my desperate questions.)

It still saddened me greatly that my father would not meet my unborn child nor would Dad meet my brother Elias' soon-to-be-born child. Our Emma Lynne was born in April 2009, seven weeks early and also breech, which meant an emergency C-section was planned during our air ambulance ride to Edmonton. She was born healthy but needed three weeks in NICU for low birth weight. I had gone off work almost three months early and it still made no difference in my premature labour onset. I took the time in the NICU to write Emma her lullaby.

It was an amazing time to bond with the newest addition to the Rumancik Crew. Shaun was at home with the other three and was finding out just how impossible it was to keep up. He couldn't believe the endless laundry and the pointlessness of cleaning the house. I rejoiced that he finally could empathize with how difficult it was to be a stay-at-home mom. His Monday to Friday day job had usually left him ignorant at how grueling Monday to Friday at home really was.

My brother Elias and his wife, Stacey, also welcomed their daughter, Hannah Maendel, just one week later.

As Shaun recited a verse during her baby dedication ceremony, it was declared that Emma would be a light in our home and she definitely through the years has proven that blessing to be true. I had asked our beloved Pastor Hayward Eastman to give Emma a special "Papa Blessing" on behalf of her Papa in heaven she would never meet here on earth.

Shaun and I had seriously talked about moving closer to home but I wasn't as eager now that my father had passed away but our parents were getting older and moving closer would mean we could be a support to each other. A big part of me loved my privacy; living twelve hours away from family was nice. Shaun and I had grown to depend on each other and we were a very close family from having moved away. I was torn: should we move or stay? I definitely did not want to leave my friends and our incredible spiritual supports found in our loving church family.

I did my best not to miss a session of the Wednesday morning Bible studies. It is extremely important for new moms to get out of the house after a baby and socialize with other moms, although this was not always easy for me as I was still struggling with many self-esteem issues and insecurities. My husband tried to be a supportive listener but didn't quite understand the depth of my hormonal issues at the time. There were days where I would be so overwhelmed by having a newborn, toddler, five year old, teenager, and two manipulative dogs. On the worst of the worst days, I will admit to calling my husband and when he would answer the call, I then would leave the phone beside a screaming Emma so that he could listen to our demanding little lamb, and would walk out of her room, leaving both her and the phone in the crib. My husband would admit to me later that he actually listened for a long time so that he then could try to be more supportive when he got home. I was thankful when he told me this for it proved that he was at least trying to nurture his attitude.

I didn't even know how to cope let alone try and explain it to my husband. Glen and Emma were very demanding in personality, much different than Bailey and Sadie. Bailey and his sister were very compliant. Glen was definitely a challenge as his antics proved daily that he had no fear. He was a bundle of fun, for sure, but you could not leave him alone for more than ten seconds.

Our pastor had encouraged us to find a prayer closet to spend time with the Lord, to find strength for the day. One day called for desperate measures and decided I would literally find a closet. Entering my room I quickly made a space in my bedroom closet and snuggled into the dark corner of the floor and closed the sliding doors. The kids were safe and I just needed so desperately to find a private place to pray. Okay, let's be honest: I was secluding myself in a quiet private space so that I could have a little mental breakdown without the eyes of my children upon me.

The tears that poured down and landed in my lap were large drops of complete hopelessness. I needed to get out of the house and had no escape. My sister who lived nearby thought I was too needy and, having never had children of her own yet, could never fathom how desperately I needed a break. So I called out to the only one who could help. I pleaded "Please, please, send someone who can help me, God. I am so desperate for someone who can understand how I feel. Please send your most empathetic person. I can't take this anymore…"

My plea was interrupted by the sound of my husband's voice in the dining room. He was home from work and I begged God, "Oh, please, anybody but him." I wanted a person who would be able to understand how I was feeling, knowing full well that my husband was not one who easily dealt with my rollercoaster of emotions. I didn't want to deal with his joking or sarcasm. As the closet door slid open and I saw Shaun's hand reach down, I slapped it away and closed the door again, telling God once more that I needed him to send me someone who could understand me the most. My spirit could not deny the Lord speaking to my heart and telling me "This is the right person." As I sat and pondered the thought that maybe my husband was sent as the perfect person, Shaun opened the closet door slowly. I soon decided to grab hold of his hand, and in one strong movement he pulled me to my feet and wrapped his arms around me.

As I released all my pride, I allowed myself to feel the security and strength in his embrace and the tears flowed once again. No words were needed for I simply enjoyed being in his strong arms. I felt the love and the security in his embrace and I thanked God for sending me just the right person. We sometimes don't realize what a gift our vulnerability can be. It was in these moments that Shaun and I continued to affirm that we truly were one.

As my anxiety level increased, I began to realize that something just didn't feel right. I knew that my post-partum struggle was in full swing but now, it seemed like I was really losing my patience even more, and I was filled with irritability and fatigue. I didn't want to brave the day's events and fight through all my shambled thoughts.

I had been to public health appointments for Emma s checkups and had completed the post-partum screening with a higher risk score than ever before. The public health nurse encouraged to seek medical attention but I had way too much fear bound up inside of me from my father's experience with anti-depressants to dare think of braving any medications. How horrible it is that fear binds us from making the proper decisions. There are lots of moments where I want to go back in time and whisper a truth to my younger self that might alter a path but I have to ask myself: would you really, Jenny? Reach back to that horrible time and possibly alter the greatest experience with Jesus ever? I tell you truthfully that as I look back I would go through the fire again because I stand stronger today for what my husband and I have persevered through.

16 RESTING IN THE LORD

WE CONCLUDED THAT 2010 WAS TO BE A GOOD YEAR AS SHAUN HAD DECIDED TO APPLY for some electrical jobs in southern Saskatchewan and he was looking forward to the job change.

Our church had also begun a new tradition and teaching on the biblical principle of fasting. In Matthew chapter 6, it is clearly stated that as a Christians there are three specific duties as spoken by Jesus Himself: giving to the needy, prayer and fasting. All of these were equal in Jesus' description of the life of a believer. Many people believe that only spiritual leaders or monks are to practice fasting but it was made clear by Jesus as he taught that fasting should be as important as prayer and giving to the needy. Our congregation had begun to incorporate a twenty-one-day fast at the beginning of the church year. As Shaun and I learned more about fasting, we began to consider joining in the fast for a week and together experience this biblical principle. We would do it together, being accountable to each other and spending time in prayer individually and together. "Fasting is something that can strengthen your walk with God and open the gates of heaven to hear God's voice more clearly," our minister had said with confidence on Sunday morning, and we all drank in this refreshing wisdom. I was excited to try this with Shaun. Both of us agreed that fasting could give us better discernment about our possible transition closer to our families. We secretly wished we were part of the military families that lived in our area who were told when they were to move.

At the same time, our home was a hub of excitement as we eagerly anticipated the arrival of my mother. She was coming to Cold Lake for a week and we were very excited to see her. The kids swarmed their Grandma as she entered our home in mid-January. When the kids were settled, my mother took no time telling me that she could see that something was wrong with my mental state. I definitely did not feel like myself and was thankful that someone finally agreed with me; she said she could see it in my eyes. My mother had never struggled with any sort of depression, hormone imbalance and definitely not post-partum depression. She could not understand how after having four kids, I couldn't just simply run a home and pull myself together but I couldn't.

My mother had only been there for one day and let's just say that it wasn't a good morning. Shaun and I were also on day three of our fast. The third day of any fast is known as one of the most challenging days but we had enjoyed our spiritual journey and had been very supportive of one another. It was a busy household as you can imagine. There was demanding little duck, Emma, who was just nine months old; her equally demanding sidekick, wild duck Glen who was just over two years old; whiny duck Sadie who was five; and big duck, Bailey Aaron who was almost fifteen. Grandma was busy trying to get Sadie ready for school, and also trying her best not to interfere with my argument with Bailey.

I had gone downstairs to the laundry room and found that Bailey had once again caused the washer to come off its base due to the way he had loaded the washer. He was pushing his attitude to the limit with me and I was getting angrier by the minute.

As a desperate means to deal with his mouthy nature (which also was being escalated because Grandma was there and he usually acted out more when she was around), I decided that I would deal with his attitude with a few smacks on the hand with a wooden spoon—I'm ashamed to admit it but I figured at the time that he was acting like a four-year-old so I would discipline him as if he was one. He was definitely not compliant and, as he tried to run for cover, I angrily shoved him and he whacked his head as he was heading for his room. As he hollered that he had hit his head, I refused to believe him as I was still furious and desperate to control the situation.

It was a *bad* morning and was definitely not the norm in our house but there was lot going on, including my approach to parenting. I am in no way saying that it was appropriate to smack a fourteen year old with a wooden spoon. As I tried to put things back together, Bailey left the house in an emotional heap.

I knew I had blown it royally and also that I had been losing my grip on my relationship with Bailey slowly over the last few months. I was not used to his defiance, his aggressive nature with his siblings, and even his aggression at school. In the last few weeks, a teacher had commented to me and Shaun that he had thought Bailey was going to lunge at him in class. I had felt that exact same way and feared Bailey's aggressive attitude as it was something that I had no coping mechanisms for. All I had ever needed was to give Bailey was a dirty look and he would comply. Shaun and I had definitely increased our physical discipline with him in the past months, for he was becoming more and more non-compliant. Of course, we could see that the change was also due to the teen years that Bailey was transitioning through, but Shaun and I were trying our best to raise a teenager alongside three children, ages five and under.

There had been lots of good things happening between Bailey and us. Shaun and Bailey had enjoyed many father-son moments and Bailey enjoyed kicking his dad's butt during their occasional chess matches in the evening. They were making eager plans for their boys' getaway to Edmonton at the end of January. We had given Bailey tickets to an Edmonton Oilers game. They would tie into the weekend's events the long awaited *Avatar 3D* movie that was in theatres at the same time. We were growing stronger as a family and trying our best to survive. I guess God had different plans as we were about to experience a godly intervention like no other.

As the day continued, I felt a sick uneasy feeling in the pit of my stomach. I went to pick up Sadie from kindergarten and on the short walk back home I gave her hand an extra squeeze and told her that I was sorry for getting so angry this morning and that I loved her and her siblings very much. That was when her sweet voice felt like the biggest sucker-punch ever. I almost doubled over when she said, "I know you love me. I told the police officer today that you were a good mommy." She then told me the rest of the story, that a lady had come to her school, had taken her out of class, had given her a stuffed animal and had told her not to be scared. Sadie was then taken to the police station where she told me she was scared and nervous until she was taken to a room where Bailey was waiting. My reality was shaken as I called Shaun in tears. We were both upset by the fact Sadie had been taken out of school. I made a phone call to the Social Services office and was politely informed that a social worker was indeed working on a case involving our family, that she would be getting in contact with me soon, that Bailey was not going to be coming home.

Shaun, my mother and I were all trying to deal with the reality of the situation and I was definitely being told by my inner voice how guilty I was, how this time I had really done it, that Bailey was gone…the thoughts were continuous.

My friend Jen randomly called me and I quickly spilled my fearful situation. I loved her honesty and our transparent relationship but this time I could have done without her honest comment, "Well, looks like you're in the system now." I couldn't argue with her and she promised to be there with whatever would play out. I hung up with the promise that I would keep her posted. I was thankful that I had friends that I could be so vulnerable with. Jen was no stranger to my stressful life and easily empathized with me while we exercised and vented about our daily stresses.

Shaun had been home for less than an hour when there was a knock at the door. I went to open the door and there was a nicely dressed young woman with a briefcase standing on the front steps asking to come in. As I moved away from the door to let her in, my eyes very quickly fell on the two police officers and another older woman also dressed in business attire behind her. My heart felt like it flipped over a few times and a cold sweat ran down my arms. She told me that she was from Social Services and that she had a court order to remove all children from our home. I backed up in disbelief as I looked frantically around the room to see where Shaun was. He had come into the living room and thought that they were some sort of sales people until he too saw the police officers. His initial thought was that it was related to Bailey; he had not heard them say they were here to apprehend all the children from our home. My mother let out a gut-wrenching scream and started yelling at the social workers that this was ridiculous. My husband stood in disbelief when they continued to inform me that I was under arrest for an assault charge on Bailey Rumancik.

I ran to the couch and grabbed nine-month-old Emma who had been in her grandmother's arms. Sadie and Glen stood in the middle of our living room, too young to understand the devastation that was going on around them. As I clung to Emma, I was calmly informed that I would be arrested by force if need be and that they did not want to use those measures in front of the children.

Handing the baby to my mother, I ran to my husband who stood stunned in the middle of the living room, grabbing his sweatshirt in both hands. I was close to ripping his shirt when he wrapped his arms around me. The officers were still telling me to come to the door for I was under arrest. I looked at my mother who had her one hand covering her mouth in shock and and the other still clinging to little Emma. The lioness in Grandma erupted as she strongly voiced that her grandchildren were not leaving this home.

It was getting close to the place where I was going to be arrested by force if I did not comply with the orders to follow the officers out of our home. I looked at Shaun one more time and quickly kissed Glen, then whispered into Sadie's ear to be brave. As I kissed her on her head, someone told us that we were not to worry, that there was a very loving home ready and waiting for our children. As I was getting my winter boots on, I heard my husband's voice in a desperate plea. "Can we go? Please. Please, we'll go instead of the kids. Please let us go, the kids can stay…" He was in shock and his words came out in short bursts.

I soon found myself in the back of a police cruiser that was parked on the street in front of our home. The officer in the car was a young female probably in her late twenties, while her partner was an older gentleman who had remained inside. It was made very clear that they were there to assist in keeping Shaun and I civil as our children were being apprehended by the social workers. I was sobbing choked grunts and holding my stomach as the beginning of shock was setting in. The lights were on in the back of the cruiser car and as I looked towards our house, I could see Sadie and Glen staring out of our large living room window right at me. I begged for her to turn out the lights in the interior, and in a cold voice she informed me she would not. She then proceeded to read me my rights and told me again that I was charged.

I was surprised to see the other social worker pacing on the front of our sidewalk as she talked on the phone. I studied her closely as she seemed to be dealing with a dilemma of some sort as she was waving her hands in a confusing manner. The police officer was still giving me details on my charge and I tried to pay attention, but I had an odd sense of relief wash over me. You couldn't get a bigger picture of someone's imprisoned state but I had a sense of freedom wash over me. I finally had everything I had ever kept closed up exposed. My anger, volatility, my desperate attempt to cope were now in the open and I felt my whole body surrender to my new circumstance. It was as if I had been hit with a wave of fresh water on a hot summer day. The realization that I was guilty helped me give up the fight. She was clearly telling me that Bailey did indeed have a bump on his head from the morning's events, one that I had helped create when I gave him a shove when he was already going down the stairs. Bailey and I both could testify that yes, both my hands were on his back giving him an extra push. My mother had tried to say that I had not but she had not witnessed the event.

It seemed I was in the back seat for so long. The officer kept talking, and I think it had something to do with showing up in court and also showing up for fingerprints. My head jolted back to reality quickly when I heard her last comment—mug shots! I was let out of the car and I was filled with an overwhelming sense of strength and peace. The |officer was speaking to the social worker and I heard her say that other arrangements had been made, that the parents were going to leave the family home and leave the children at home with the grandmother. I was stunned as I was allowed back in the house. Shaun quickly confirmed that my sister was on her way and that she and my mother would now be left in the care of our kids. What an amazing change of events. My spirit leaped as the senior social worker rudely stated that there would still be a Catholic social worker volunteer coming to spend the night at our home, and that the necessary paperwork would then be filed in the morning. Shaun and I tried to grab the most necessary things and left our home while the police stood guard. If you're wondering if the TV episodes are accurate on how they portray these events, I can tell you they are almost identical to what happens in real life.

As Shaun and I were sitting in the truck in the driveway, the cold January night air soon covered us. We shivered in shock as we were trying to come to our senses. All we knew was that we had an appointment at the Social Services the very next day. Shaun was swearing under his breath in total disbelief, still stunned that he had found the courage or the quick response to request that we leave instead of our children. I was completely convinced that very night that I had married a knight in shining armour. My husband was a man of character who had saved us all from an even more disastrous situation. Shaun and I could never have endured watching our children being forcefully taken from our home. As we drove out of our driveway, I heard my husband say, "Where are we supposed to go now?" I immediately responded with the answer, "We have to go to our pastor's home." We could not endure this situation alone. Shaun only hesitated a few moments before he drove across town. We called them prior to arriving and discussed briefly our desperate situation.

My friend Cindy greeted us at the front door, quickly ushering us into a quiet area of the house and embracing us in an emotional hug. Cindy held me tightly as I wept uncontrollably. Shaun and Pastor Lance did the same. The shock of the evening's events had left us all confused and broken. They very quickly prayed and a lawyer attending the church was called. The lawyer stated that these events can be very traumatic but said that the next day would be better. We were encouraged to let the dust settle.

Pastor Lance then did the first of many God-driven things. He grabbed Shaun's hand and shaped it into a fist he then grabbed mine and placed it over top of Shaun's. Then, with a strong force, he said, "I don't know what all to say but I feel God telling me this: Trust God! Trust God! Do not separate in any moment while you are dealing with this situation. Stay as one, try not to argue or blame but remember to remain as one." His words were strong and strengthening. They were sealed with confirmation every time he pounded our hands together. I will never forget that moment.

As Cindy filled us a care package, we were soon given a church-funded hotel room for the night. As Cindy embraced me one last time she told me that I should have hope. She later said she would never forget the look of complete hopelessness that I had in my eyes when I first arrived.

When Shaun and I arrived at the hotel and plunked ourselves down on the bed, we both could feel the shock and disbelief take its physical toll; we were exhausted. Shaun decided to phone his parents and inform them of the situation we now found ourselves in. As his voice began to crack, it was clear to me that he was talking to his father. I moved to a quiet place away from my husband and gave him his space to have the heart-to-heart with his father. Shaun and his dad had become close since we moved and Shaun had even received a verbal blessing from his father. Shaun referred to his father as his super hero. I was thankful that our relationship had strengthened with his parents since moving to Alberta. I felt a strong sense that there was a war raging in the heavenly realm, that God was working hard on our behalf and this word from our minister to trust God was very real. I grabbed a notepad and wrote long and hard in desperation, seeking answers from God—why this? This was too huge of a situation to endure, and it didn't make any sense that all the kids would need to be involved. The fact that they thought we had a dangerous house was too much to take.

As we both tried to sleep, we had high hopes that our meeting with Children's Services the next day would end this crazy situation we found ourselves in. I was also experiencing a great deal of pain in my upper body as I lay in bed weeping—no one had even taken the time to consider the truth that Emma was a breastfed baby. In all the shock it hadn't crossed my mind either until now, and the physical pain was becoming increasingly too much.

The next morning Shaun and I awoke to find our truck had a flat tire. How would it look if we were late for our meeting to fight for our family? What else could go possibly wrong? As Shaun struggled to deal with the tire, I just kept thinking that we couldn't handle much more. As we sat outside the office doors in the small waiting room, we found ourselves deep in conversation at how we would react to the many questions that we would likely be asked. Shaun had a strong sense that we as a family had nothing to hide so we would continue forward with the complete truth. Whatever they asked us we would answer accordingly.

As we were sitting there, Shaun's cell phone rang. As he spoke I could tell it was not someone we knew well and Shaun found himself at a loss for words. He handled the call as best as he could and looked completely broken when he got off the phone. I sat stunned when he told me it was a call from the electrical job that he had applied for just a few weeks earlier. "How am I supposed to consider this job interview when I don't even have my family all together?" My heart broke for my husband and, as I sat there, fear gripped my every bone. Waiting was brutal.

Finally the doors swung open and we were greeted by the same social worker as the night before. We were then informed that we would both be questioned separately. Again we both were stunned as we had not even considered the fact that we could be going into this alone. We were each in with the social worker for an hour and both of us told the complete truth; there was not one stupid thing we had done as parents that we did not admit. I didn't care anymore—I was completely exposed in every area of my life. It was also incredible to find out that Bailey had given them six years of information on every detail of our lives, every fight, and every embarassing detail of our hardest days. Bailey had been a witness to all our toughest years. I was hurt that he seemed to be on such a mission to give them as much dirt on his mother as possible. I knew that Bailey was convinced that his life would be better if he lived at his friend's house. Who could blame him as this home did not have any strict rules and no young siblings. It was a quiet home where a mother and son lived a content life. But I lost my bitterness for my son's informative mission by the end of my session with the social worker. I couldn't imagine how difficult it would be for any child to go through a session like this with any social worker.

After the individual sessions, Shaun and I once again found ourselves together in the waiting area. We were exhausted and both could not imagine how Bailey or Sadie could have endured such questioning.

It didn't take long and we soon sat in the meeting room facing the social workers, a supervisor and the two that we met the night before. The supervisor spoke first. "We knew exactly what kind of parents you both were as soon as you chose to leave your home!" He then informed us that they deal with many parents who usually abandon their children in the shock of these kind of events. Shaun and I could definitely understand how the shock of the previous night could easily have caused fear and abandonment. He confirmed that he had never seen parents do what we had done spontaneously, uprooting ourselves. My spirit leaped as he spoke for now I knew what was going on in the heavenly realm on our behalf. It was so true what the minister had said about fasting being a very spiritual experience. God had indeed been there the night before and had made sure we were validated as parents as soon as we passed the threshold of our very own front door.

They told us it was concerning how much physical discipline was used in our home. The fact that they had planted an assault charge on me from my incident with Bailey made it clear that this was not going to be resolved soon. As Shaun and I sat there, numb and weak, they informed us we needed some parenting classes and anger management, among other things related to stress management, and that they would be arranging these courses for us.

Then they announced that we had lost custody of all of our children for a total of three months. I couldn't hold my emotions together any longer and I became angry, telling them this was ridiculous. My husband agreed. We did not think that a wooden spoon used for a smack on the hand was appropriate and agreed that it was ridiculous that we had chosen to use physical discipline on Bailey due to his increase in difficult behaviour—but they were taking this too far. We had done the things that would classify us as parents who chose harsh means of discipline—like smacking Glen's bare butt for repeatedly doing cannonballs while in the bathtub. As Shaun tried to plead our case, he stated that we were not denying the fact that we were in need of some intervention but that removing our children from us was only going to make this worse. We would willingly comply with all their expectations but we pleaded desperately to be back with our children.

There was no change in their stoic expressions so Shaun blasted them with a dose of reality. I have to admit that I enjoyed the shocked look on all their faces when my husband said, "We need to see our children as soon as possible because Jenny has not breastfed Emma in almost twenty-four hours. This is causing my wife a great physical discomfort." They quickly assured us that we could return to our home shortly but that visits would be supervised by a worker.

My mother and my sister were approved as the primary caregivers of our children while in our home. Shaun was encouraged to return to work as soon as possible as this was going to be our new normal. We had supervised visitations planned for every day from five to seven p.m., to ensure that I could breastfeed Emma every evening before she settled for the night. Shaun asked if it was possible to see Bailey as soon as possible. They agreed to arrange this and then informed us that the police officer had brought Bailey back home from his friend's house as soon as we had driven out of our yard (his plan hadn't even gotten him one night away from home). We left the room feeling very defeated and shocked that this was indeed our new normal. Our home had become a foster home. And we were homeless.

As we entered our home, I could see the stress on my mother's face. She looked drained and still baffled at all the events. As she held me and we wept together, we concluded that our faith in God would see us through. My mother could not fathom what would have happened had she not been in Cold Lake. I shuddered at the thought and couldn't bring myself to think further about what could have been. My sister was in full swing, being a happy distraction to her nieces and nephews, and we were so thankful that she was there to nurture them. Shaun and I caught each other's eyes in our total disbelief at the situation we found ourselves in. I tried to breastfeed Emma and was thankful for the relief but found it difficult to manage in the time-frame we now had.

The volunteer worker had spent the night and was also still present. I instantly felt the warmth of her demeanour and wrapped my arms around her neck when she told me that she had been shocked when she arrived the night before to find a loving cozy home, and she could not make sense of what must have happened to bring all this on. I knew the answer but kept my mouth shut. I felt it had all greatly been blown out of proportion. This volunteer worker was a welcome comfort to all of us as we had lots of questions about how this was all going to work out. Shaun and I made arrangements to meet privately with Bailey after school the very next day. As our time was up, we left our home once again and said our tearful goodbyes. Glen was screaming and couldn't understand why he couldn't come with us. My husband's emotions were very raw as curse words rolled off his tongue. How would we ever survive this ordeal?

Astonishingly enough, my sister had agreed to house sit for a search-and-rescue pilot who had been attending our church and who had gone to Haiti to help with the disaster that had hit Haiti the same date that our disaster had hit and practically around the same time. (I am in no way comparing our situation with the catastrophic earthquake or tsunami; I simply found it astonishing that our situations were all happening on the same day and almost exact same time.) Since the search-and-rescue pilot had two pets to care for, it was necessary for someone to live at the residence in his absence. My sister got in touch with the pilot and explained our situation, and he very quickly agreed that Shaun and I could stay in place of my sister. We were overwhelmed with the fact that this complete stranger would be so gracious to us. We were very thankful that we didn't have to rent a hotel room for three months. Once again we were surrounded by God's goodness, and so it was that my sister traded places with the two of us.

There was no way that Shaun could conceive of going back to work immediately but we agreed that he would return after we had established some normalcy. We found a lawyer and approached her with our situation. She informed us that because my court date was scheduled for a few months away, Social Services had leeway to stretch out our ordeal. She encouraged us to come up with an action plan and to comply as best as possible with all they asked of us. She also graciously ensured us that she would give us any legal support we needed at no charge. Once again we were so grateful for the kindness she showed. She encouraged us further when she told us that, when she had worked in a bigger law firm in her former practice, there were many files on families in the same situation as we were, most of which had been brought on by an angry teenager.

Shaun and I were getting settled into our new surroundings. The pilot's house was in one of the more high-end neighbourhoods, and it was new and cozy. It was a nice distraction for us to have two kind dogs to care for and they seemed to be grateful to us, too.

We had requested a private meeting with just Bailey prior to our evening visit. The social worker was going to be picking him up from school as she would then supervise our little meeting. Our social worker was young and tried her best to be kind but I was becoming angrier by the moment at the thought that someone had more rights to my son than I had, that she could have the freedom that I used to have. I felt overwhelmed with emotions that my bond with my son had been taken from me. Bailey and I had always shared a very close bond and it was crumbling quickly as I was powerless.

As we heard Bailey enter our home, I quickly regained my strength, and snapped out of my irritation. When Bailey came into the room, we noticed how awful he looked. His eyes had dark circles under them and his face was as green as I had ever seen. We were standing and the social worker said a few words and then handed the floor over to us. Shaun approached Bailey first and asked him if he had gotten the outcome he expected. To this, Bailey answered, "I just don't want you guys to use physical discipline on me anymore." Shaun vowed to him that he would never use such discipline again. He then proceeded to tell Bailey that he loved him and that since his own father had not sworn at him when he called and gave him the news of our incident, then he too would not curse Bailey in any way either. He forgave and hugged him.

It was my turn but I found it difficult to speak. Never mind one frog in my throat—it felt like there were two or three. I choked out some words asking him how he was coping and then embraced him and told him that I loved him. When Bailey replied that he loved me also, I said something that caught me off guard: "I don't believe you!" I realized I still thought I was unworthy of my son. How could he love me for all the tight-gripped parenting I had put him through? We talked a short while longer and then left our home, feeling a little lighter than when we came. We decided to debrief before completing our evening visit with the other children.

***

It was Monday morning and we were almost a week into our new situation. Shaun decided to return to work and I definitely was not going to stay in the house alone without Shaun I decided to go to the gym. There I had such a strong presence of Jesus being with me.

My friend Jen and I had enjoyed the new indoor facilities together often, so I was well acquainted with all this place had to offer. The Cold Lake Energy Centre was a beautiful new facility with an indoor soccer field and an upper level walking track and of course a spacious workout area. In the corner of the upper level walking track was a place with some tables and chairs, a perfect place to sit and journal. So as Shaun left for work at 6 a.m., I decided that I would go to the only place I found comfort: the gym. I found myself with a fresh Timmies in one hand and my Bible and journal in the other. As I laced up my running shoes, I could feel the pressure building. I shrugged off the tears stinging the corners of my eyes and took a deep breath. I would find the strength to survive another day.

As I began to walk the track I prayed, asking God to please help me endure the pain of my breaking heart and the cruel thoughts constantly telling me that I was a hopeless cause and a bad mother. I didn't make it around the first loop before I felt the strongest sense that I was not alone. As I looked around, it was clear that I was the only one on the walking track and on the third floor. I felt a strong sense of peace and warmth flood my soul and began to pray even more intimately. I cannot recall my exact words, but I do remember the desperate plea that came out of my being when my tears poured afresh and faith turned to cold fear. "Lord why this? Why did this have to happen? I don't understand all of this. It's too much; I can't bear the pain."

As my emotions erupted in uncontrollable sobs, I heard him as clear as ever. He spoke right to my heart. It wasn't an audible voice but a still, small voice, like it states in Scripture. His voice echoed with tenderness and compassion, and I will never forget his words: "Jenny, I need you to heal, and in order for you to do this I had to take your biggest distractions away, your children." I was overcome with his response. It was clear and precise, and I was in awe. As I allowed all my fears to melt away, I began to believe in what he had said.

With Jesus by my side, I walked and jogged my way around the track. He never left me. He was there now, right there with me at the gym. I had no idea of the confirmation that would soon come my way.

In fact, for the whole duration of our ordeal, Jesus was with me every morning as I worked out my frustrations at the gym. He never left my side and I had never felt his presence as strongly. The protective covering was all-consuming. His pace was my pace. As I walked, I regained more strength than I thought I could own. It was there that both my body and mind were made ready for the battle at hand.

This tender fitness trainer was like none other and he charged me absolutely no membership fee. He encouraged me and allowed me the freedom to rest and heal. When it was time to run, He would run; when it was time to cry I felt His warmth even stronger. He reassured me that this was a time of rebuilding my spiritual body and that He had all of life's other problems under control. He knew that I had always longed to get to the gym and had given me the open-ended situation to take all the time I needed. I had often desired to hire a fitness trainer after having my young children but now I fully understood why that was definitely not necessary. I am all for a fitness trainer but He knew what I really needed was a spiritual coach named Jesus. To be made whole. Me and Jesus working out—this was my training camp so that I could run the race He had set before me in life and run it well! I could truly say that I met Jesus at the gym.

During my morning devotions, I tried to brainstorm how I was going to spend my days. I definitely was not interested in seeing anyone I knew, for Shaun and I felt we were in hideout in our very own city. Cindy had called one of our prayer intercessors and discussed our situation with her. She worked with some city programs and was also working on her counselling certificate, mostly in the life coaching area. I was in agreement with her involvement and began seeing her almost immediately. I had never heard of a life coach before but it sounded like something I needed.

But I could only imagine what our neighbours alone were thinking as I was sure they had seen all the events involving a police car in our front yard. I tried not to think about who knew and who didn't. I couldn't even imagine how Shaun felt because he was a complete introvert. I had decided to contact my friend Danielle—she definitely needed to hear it from me before she heard it anywhere else. There were only three people I was willing to discuss my vulnerability with: Danielle, Cindy and Jen.

As I called Danielle and set up a time where we could meet for coffee, I told her it would be an evening out at Tim Hortons, just her and me. When she arrived at the coffee shop, she greeted me warmly and chatted about what a great idea it was to get out of the house and away from the kids. I thought, *You have no idea, my friend.* It didn't take long for me to pour out all the gruesome details that we had been facing. Tears poured down my friend's face as she listened with complete shock. I could tell that she was devastated and that I didn't need to ever prove to her that I was indeed a good mother and would be dying to have my children back, especially a child as young as Emma. We finished up our chat and my friend left for home with swollen red eyes.

One day during my early morning at the gym, a thought crossed my mind: I wondered if it could be possible to spend some time at Sadie's school. I called to verify the idea with our case worker and she promised to look into my idea. Before long I was allowed to walk into Sadie's class as a parent volunteer. The look on my daughter's face when I arrived in her class each day was priceless, and I was so thankful we shared those weeks together. I felt badly when some of the kids in her class would comment, "I wish my mommy would come to my class every day!" I couldn't help but silently say to myself, "Your mommy would only have to be charged and arrested in order to share this privilege with you." I didn't chuckle long but found it hard to console those little lambs. So my routine was that I spent my early hours at the gym and the bigger chunk of my day at Sadie's school. Of course I made sure I wasn't anywhere near at the end of the day because I was forbidden to take my daughter home from school. How humiliating.

Within the first week, I informed Shaun of something very important: we should not take any of this time for granted. We had never had a season to be alone, truly alone, and now here we were in a beautiful home, in one of the nicer areas of town and a court order that we were only allowed to see our children for two hours every evening, and a little longer on weekends. So we made a pact that we would treat it as a honeymoon like no other.

One day, someone approached me and my worst fears became a reality. They knew some of the facts but misunderstood them. I had finally braved going into a shopping centre and had a plan to get in and get out before anyone who knew me spotted me. Well, my plan failed greatly and this person was determined to find out the truth. She told me that she had read about us on Facebook (our neighbours indeed were sending out inaccurate information), and my knees buckled as her words came at me. This person had no idea the impact her words had on me as she genuinely had care and concern. I politely excused myself and walked away as fast as my trembling legs could take me.

With the safe confines of my vehicle, I let out a scream of complete horror. I wanted to vomit with the ideas that could be planted in people's minds like that. Shaun was as furious as I was and felt sick and angered at the power the government agency held over us.

We were at a loss for where to turn when our ministers encouraged us to bring it before the church. Shaun feared that I would bolt from this situation and leave him to deal with it all alone. As he held me and we both sobbed great tears, he begged, "Please don't leave me—I can't do this alone." It was clear to us, as our minister had told us, that we were never to separate, that we were to stay as one.

We found ourselves at our pastor's home again for some much needed spiritual encouragement. We were surrounded with loving hugs and kind words. It was clear that they were not only our ministers but also our dear friends. We all agreed that Shaun and I would share our situation with our congregation on Sunday.

Walking into our church had never been scary before but was definitely terrifying to both of us that day. We had avoided our church the previous Sunday and had gone to another town for Sunday morning worship. We were easily nauseated by the innocent question, "Where are your kids?"

Our senior minister has an amazing way with words and can sum up any situation with just a few sentences, a gift I wish I had more often. That Sunday morning, our pastor began by encouraging all those who were continuing on with the twenty-one-day fast. Then he said his next perfectly spoken words. "You know that we as a church have been celebrating many breakthroughs and miracles in the past few weeks, and that's awesome!" He paused slightly as if to regain control over his emotions. "Sometimes, though, during a fast there are tremendous trials that some of us will face, and we have a family within our church family that is enduring one of these trials right now." *Here we go*, I thought, about to crumble, "If you know Shaun and Jenny Rumancik, they would like you to stay after the morning service while they share just what trials they are facing." As he finished and worship began, I squeezed Shaun's hand harder and said how beautifully that had been put.

The service ended, and Shaun and I became a bundle of nerves. Amazingly, about fifty people stayed after the service. Every one of them we considered our close church family. As Shaun stood up in front of the church with our pastor right beside him, it was Pastor Lance who began the introduction to the beautiful gathering. He made it clear that this was a private matter and a very vulnerable family situation for both Shaun and me.

As he handed the floor over to Shaun, my heart broke at how hard this must be for my shy, quiet husband. I prayed desperately that he would be able to handle the pressure. As he began to speak, he was clear that he was the leader and the defender of the Rumancik Crew. He said that we had had an incident involving our teenager a few weeks back which had led us to lose all our children to the care of Social Services. My heart welled up with love that he had spoken of us as a joint team when it was clear to me that it had been an incident that I alone had had with our teenager. He made it very clear that we did not want to discuss the details but wanted our friends and family to hear about it from us. There were many tears and gasps of disbelief. Shaun spoke with clarity and strength and handed the floor back to our minister who said the most beautiful words in closing. "What Shaun and Jenny have been accused of every one of us has done in our families." He was definitely not implying that our congregation was full of child abusers, but confirming that every one of us has crossed the line with the anger and frustration that comes from stresses within a family home.

Our church family then formed two lines, one in front of Shaun and one in front of me, and they all embraced us and prayed with us and cried with us. It was an amazing experience! Jesus made it clear when He said, "*I am the light of the world. Whoever follows me will never walk in darkness, but will have the light of life*" (John 8:12, NIV).Shaun and I had brought our situation into the light, and the power that Satan had was diminished by the love of our Saviour, as proven by the act of love from our church family. Our church family began to also drop off suppers at our family home to support my mother and sister. There would also be gifts and treats dropped off for our children. Shaun and I were so thankful as we were all beginning to feel the financial crunch from our family situation. We also felt the pressures of the evening visits and had not heard from our social worker in three weeks. We contacted our social worker to see if there were any courses that we had been registered for and were notified that she hoped to be providing us with that information within a few days.

So life continued on in our new normal: Shaun went to work, I had my time with Sadie at school, I met with my life coach, and I met Jesus at the gym each day and was sure that He was always in attendance as His presence in my life was becoming more real every day.

I had a brand new outlook on all the things I could now let go of in my life. My priorities were clearer: God, Jenny, Shaun, Children. I learned about the importance of self-care, and strategies to convince my family to let me have some time alone. Things were not as hard as they were before we met with our church family. I had a new peace and sense of strength that God was taking care of my every need. Shaun and I were persevering as a team and taking every opportunity to enjoy our time alone together. My friend Jen had also been helping at getting me out of 'my woe is me' state of mind. One day when I was lamenting about all we were enduring and was trying to figure out God in our entire situation, Jen came straight to the point. "Jenny!" she said both sternly and with love. "God's not here—he's in Haiti!" I laugh as much now as I did then. Jen didn't profess a faith nor did she go to church but she believed in Jesus and she was right that I could also consider people who were suffering much greater things than I could ever imagine. We kept forgetting the devastation in the wider world.

By the end of January, Shaun and I were getting used to our ordeal, the kids seemed to be handling it better as we had some fun swimming outings at the military base's indoor pool, supervised, of course. The pool was a big part of our family's recreational activities and one we enjoyed. Bailey had been thriving since he joined the swim team and we were thankful for the outlet. We still continued to get much support from our friends. Our strength came from God and the continuous reminder we received from our friends in Christ. Here is one such letter;

Dear Shaun and Jenny

We love your family so much. Cold Lake is a better place for you living here. Every life you touch you leave remnants of his love. We are standing with you and are doing whatever it takes to get through this season. We have the same questions in our hearts: God, why and why this way, to which we hear, "My grace is sufficient for you." God says, look at the Israelites; was it not in captivity that they became strong and a very threat to their enemies? He will never allow more than you can bear. When you've done all you can to stand he will make you stand. You do your part and he will do his. I see such confidence coming on you both as you know who you are in Christ, righteousness.

"Taste and see that the Lord is good; blessed is the one who takes refuge in him" (Psalm 34:8, NIV)

"My Presence will go with you, and I will give you rest" (Exodus 33:14, NIV)

Jeremiah 17:7-8

Cindy Steeves

Meditating on all the truths of God's Word was crucial. Thankfully I was also brave enough to attend Bible study on Wednesday mornings and it was after one of our Esther sessions that I would receive the most unbelievable gift from God. This gift would give me tremendous confirmation of my walk with Jesus and especially my time at the gym. I was leaving the church one Wednesday after Bible study when I heard my name being called. As I turned, I recognized my sweet friend Janean. She was one of the Bible study leaders and had taught me much about trusting God. As she ran up to me, she handed me some papers folded in letter style, saying that she had something for me from God. At first I just thought she had written out some inspirational words but when I opened it, I became astonished. I had not spoken to her of any details surrounding the events of our lives. I was still slightly skeptical but that would all soon disappear once I got a chance to read the words:

January 25, 2010

In the light of the season, in the heart of the time, I will surely carry you upon my shoulders; you will look back upon my Grace and have revelation of my love and power. Rest in me, Rest in my judgments, comfort yourself in the Lord. Surely I have not forsaken or forgotten, surely all things shall come to completion and wholeness. Test me and prove me, Jenny. I desire to be your whole life, your purpose and your destiny. I will never leave you or forsake my chosen—only seasons change and growth will begin again. Valleys are where fruit grows and valleys are perfected and only in me is true joy. I desire wholeness for you even more than you desire your children, Rest, Jenny, I have everything under control.

Love, your Father

I very quickly read the second letter.

January 27, 2010

Despite what appears to be, I will make a way for you and Shaun. I desire that you and Shaun join together in agreement for your children's lives. You must believe and surely I will change every mindset, every hindrance, whatever stands in your way. I know that this is a hard test, perhaps the hardest one yet, but I'm in control and have never stopped being in control. Do not question my judgment, but trust that I will truly work all things for good. Your flesh will try to dissuade you and at times you will succumb *to worry, but you must persevere and firmly decide to plant your feet upon me…the Solid Rock. You may have to decide to do this multiple times a day, but as you do I will cause your heart to believe what I have already promised and you will see my hard work on your behalf, making all things whole again. Jenny, I know your heart and have withheld some things for your benefit. How is this you ask? Sometimes if I answer a prayer before a heart is ready, my answer to their prayers could literally destroy them, so then I must pursue them in a different way, still answering their prayers but preparing their heart to contain the blessing and to have no doubt that it was I who came through for them. Perhaps that seems harsh or out of perspective for a good God, but I desire that none should perish, but all have eternal life. I have promised to never leave you or forsake you, but in that there will be tests for all my chosen ones. Do not think for a moment that you are the only one because right now I am purifying all of my bride all over the world. You will begin to see more wrong things exposed, more wrong accusations, everything being brought to the surface so that my great harvest might come in. My Bride is not ready and that is why I am purging and purifying her, so that nothing will stand in the way of her testimony or my glory. I have chosen you, Jenny, for a purpose and have a specific destiny planned for you. All of your desires will be met, but first I must be enough, truly enough. Then I will open up the heavens and <u>pour out</u> my blessing, so much so that you will look back with tears of joy at how much blessing has come of this situation. I love you so much, Jenny. Your Father. I love you.*

I told Janean how incredibly confirming the letters were in what had taken place in our lives in the last year. She said she was astonished herself when she realized how much both letters confirmed each other. She said that when she felt the nudging to pen the letters, she couldn't stop writing. I have read these letters many times in the past five years and am always in awe of them. It wasn't until I began this writing project that I remembered all too clearly the desperation I felt when I wrote my letters to heaven as a child, addressed to my Heavenly Father. Now He was writing me back and at the perfect time.

These letters have confirmed many miracles in our family and I still longed to discover my specific destiny. These letters also confirmed that I was not wrong when I felt Jesus present with me that first morning at the gym and thanks to our short fast, also hearing His voice with such spiritual clarity, when Jesus confirmed, "Jenny, I need you to heal and in order for you to heal, I needed to take your biggest distraction away—your children." There was also the confirmation I received just before our ordeal when I was told I would be going through a season where I had to rest in the Lord.

MUG SHOTS

AFTER THIRTY-FOUR DAYS, THE PHONE CALL FINALLY CAME TO ARRANGE FOR SHAUN
and I to meet again with the social workers and discuss potential courses that
they had for us to take. Shaun and I had our action plan all typed up. It included
everything we had been doing for the last thirty-four days. We felt strong even
though we knew our ordeal was long from over. The court order was for a three-
month period and my first court date was scheduled for late March. We were
hopeful, though, and had learned much about ourselves, our faith, and our
friends and family. I had loved my time with my life coach and had learned so
much about myself and my relationship with Bailey.

As Shaun and I walked through the doors of Social Services, though, we
began to feel the hopelessness that we had felt at the beginning. We also couldn't
forget the times when we had dropped off numerous letters pleading for us to be
reunited with our children. We sat in the same chairs and watched for the same
doors to open. It didn't take long before we were greeted by our social worker.
We had built a relationship with her in the last month and we exchanged kind
greetings. Once in the meeting room, the supervisor proceeded to greet us and
ask us how we were managing. I don't quite think he was ready for Shaun's
quick cheerful response, "We've been managing just fine. We've never had so
much sex. We are enjoying our quality alone time and the fact that you helped
give my mother-in-law a court order to babysit our kids for a whole month has
helped give us a much-needed break." We all seemed to be amused by Shaun's
forwardness. I was a little shocked by his openness but, as Shaun stated later, they
already knew all the details about us so we might as well keep up the openness
of our relationship.

The supervisor continued by stating that they had some courses and workshops scheduled for us that they would like to go over. Shaun asked if we could present them with our own action plan, things we had been working on in the past few weeks. The supervisor agreed and Shaun began to explain it all. He described how I had been seeing a life coach from the very beginning, the parenting classes that we had signed ourselves up for, the counselling we had been receiving with our ministers, the anger management course we had signed up for, books we were reading (recommended by the life coach) and the daily volunteer hours that I was doing in our daughter's kindergarten class.

The supervisor looked astonished and asked if we would excuse them for a few minutes. Shaun and I looked at each other and felt proud of how much we had accomplished. It didn't take long before they returned and, before all of them were seated back in their chairs, the supervisor confidently said, "You can both return to your home and be reunited with your children." Shaun and I were shocked—we were definitely not expecting such results. They said that they were certain that keeping us from our children was only causing our family unnecessary stresses. We would still have to have the social worker stop in to do periodic checks to ensure we didn't need further supports. They also presented us with some workshops on raising teens, some family therapy sessions free of charge, and an evaluation for Bailey.

We were very thankful as we walked out of the office and quickly told Grandma and Aunty Anna the great news. We celebrated with praises to our Saviour Jesus as we phoned our prayer support team. News went quickly that our ordeal with Social Services was now over. We knew we still had to deal with the courts and feared that I would have a criminal record but we had hope that all would be well and God had brought us home again with our kids. There was great celebration!!

Shaun and I completed our anger management course and enjoyed our two-day information-filled course. The facilitators were very interesting and we learned a lot. I especially loved watching Shaun learn that growing up in either a volatile home or a sarcastic or cynical family were both versions of an angry home. I appreciated that we learned about how much body language accounted for in verbal communications. It was clear that we both differed greatly in how we perceived body language during our communication. We found grace for people who had stress-filled life and found the stress mapping component extremely beneficial. We had so much clarity on how to avoid future issues regarding anger and stress. The raising teens course was in Edmonton and our social workers booked us into the most beautiful room we had ever seen. We thanked them greatly when we returned home from the enjoyable learning event.

The transition home was very difficult as we had to return to the routines that we had been relieved from. My mother was finally able to return home (and thankfully had not experienced financial setbacks as she received foster care benefits for caring for our children). My sister also returned to her regular life with no penalties for having been with our family. We thanked her for assisting us through our family crisis. Bailey, Shaun and I went to Bailey's appointment where it was confirmed to us that Bailey was suffering with occasional depression, and that his aggression was likely due to the increase in his medication. I felt sick to my stomach and wished I had listened to my inner voice. I couldn't believe that we had a chemical explanation for his increase in defiant and aggressive behaviour. I am not against medications but I feel that there is a season to be on them and a season to no longer need them. Shaun and I felt ill at the fact that we had not recognized that Bailey's flat affect and expressions were signs of depression—we had taken them as a form of defiance. As we drove home I couldn't stop recalling that Bailey and I had decided to increase his dosage in mid-December which had likely been the cause for all the unexpected aggression.

Shaun was trying to poke fun at the fact that I had to be at the police station the following day for fingerprints. I couldn't believe that I still had to go through with this, and complained to God that I couldn't understand why I needed mug shots. It didn't make sense to me. I understood that I had a court date and was still facing a charge but it still seemed unnecessary to me. I would have to miss Wednesday morning Bible study to go get mug shots!

I remembered a conversation that I had had with my brother Conrad as he was trying to make jokes about his older sister going to prison. I didn't think he was funny and argued back, "I'm innocent until proven guilty!" I still appreciated his call and knew that my brothers had been very concerned.

It was a short drive to the station and I debated sitting in the vehicle to avoid it a little longer. I was thankful that no one really knew that this was the day I was getting this done. I was more irritated than emotional and felt I could brave this without any emotional breakdowns; after all, I was sick of crying! As I climbed out of my vehicle and entered the station, a wind of fear seemed to hit me, but as I handed her my paperwork, the receptionist seemed unaffected by the fact that I was about to be marked as a criminal. It didn't take long before I was ushered through the station by a very kind officer. I was numb and solemn but appreciated his kindness. *Here we go*, I thought as we rounded the corner where the bars were clearly visible. We were heading to a small room where the ink was likely waiting to smudge the guilt into the proof they needed that I was a criminal. *Yes, here I am,* I thought. *I'm thirty-three years old with four children and a career as a nurse—mug shots will go perfectly on my list of accomplishments.* I could feel God was still there and saying to me in that still small voice, "Trust me, Jenny. I'm here, I love you."

As we entered this brightly lit white room, a cold chill ran through my spine and I was thankful that I had reached out and touched the bars on my way by as a reminder to never allow myself to get here again. I was going be able to handle this, I encouraged myself silently. The officer was instructing me on the fingerprints and I felt like I was about to vomit as my stomach was doing flips. As he reached for my right hand and placed my first finger on the pad, my body began to shake and enormous tears began pouring down my face. He seemed to be concerned with my emotional breakdown and asked me if I was all right. I was so thankful for his kindness, and nodded that I was okay, although that was a lie. As he pressed all ten of my fingers into the cold wet ink and placed my prints on paper, I was in a full-on emotional breakdown. He asked me if I had ever done this before. *Are you kidding me?* I thought, and without a second thought, I quickly and shockingly answered, "No! Do I look like I have done this before?" He asked me a few more times if I was okay and if I was in any pain. I felt badly that he was at a loss for how to help but he could never understand how horrible this moment was for me.

The scariest thing I had to face was this proof on file that I had been arrested for assault on one of my children. I knew, convicted or not, these events could be accsessed at the push of a button. I was informed than I could request to have the mug shots destroyed if the charges were dropped but it did not make me feel better.

Later I came up with a little piece of comfort, remembering that Jesus himself was arrested although He was was completely innocent. I definitely was not innocent, as an assault charge is defined as one placing their hands on another in an attempt to harm. But if He had been arrested today, Jesus likely would have been subjected to mug shots and fingerprints too. It gave me some comfort that Jesus had also walked this scary road. I definitely knew He had been treated far worse than I could ever imagine. There was no comparison in our situations other than that He would also have been booked into the criminal code. It gave me the peace I needed to be vulnerable.

That evening I went to attend the make-up session for the Esther Bible study. This book had fascinated me from the beginning; it was proof that God works powerfully behind the scenes of our lives. This book begins with a biblical beauty contest like no other, choosing and preparing a new queen. The king did not realize that his new queen, Esther, was of Jewish descent, at a time when the Jewish people were subject to total annihilation due to a conspiracy by a highly appointed official to the king. Queen Esther was asked by her cousin Mordecai to go before the king and beg him to save her people. Esther fasted and sought out the Lord's strength; she also asked her maids and all the Jewish people to fast and pray with her. This story is beautiful and dramatic: her people are saved and vengeance is brought upon the king's high official.

That day's session of the Esther Bible study just so happened to be on the very part of the story where Esther had to take courage and go before the king. Beth Moore's question to all of us was this, "What would your reaction be if you had to face your most difficult and scary situation? How would you take courage?" I sat there thinking to myself how fitting it was that I had missed Wednesday morning Bible study to go and have fingerprints and mug shots taken. It gave me a perfect answer to her question. Emotional breakdown or not, I had conquered it and walked out of there with the words of Jesus in my letters. He would make all things right again and bring much blessing to this situation. I had decided to trust God that my outcome was all for a greater purpose. I chose to have faith no matter what and to love and trust Him. When someone asks me where my faith comes from, I simply can tell them that I got mug shots!

Soon, our court date approached. Shaun and I will never forget the humility that came with that experience. It would be an all-day event as it went according to alphabetical order and Rumancik would be toward the end of that order. Just as the kind-hearted lawyer had told us, she was there to support us at no charge at all. We would not accomplish anything that first date, as expected, and had to make a few more appearances. At the next date, as Shaun and I waited outside the court office, my husband grabbed my hands and prayed, thanking God for His goodness and sovereignty through all that we had been through, and to ask God to help us also through this.

As we walked in and met with our probation officer, she took us personally to the Crown Attorney with our files in hand to plead our case. Shaun and I were ready to face another long day in court. When the door opened, she ushered us in to his office and introduced us to the Crown Attorney. He had a rich French accent and looked very busy with his desk full of that day's court files. She spoke assertively to the attorney. "These are the Rumanciks as I have outlined in section…" They went into a lot of legal details. She handed him a piece of paper that showed all that we would have to accomplish as part of our legal matter. Thanks to the action plan that we had given her at the last court date, she was explaining that we had already accomplished the measures required and that we were back home with our children.

What the Crown Attorney said next I will cherish forever, like I needed any more proof that Jesus was in charge of our mission. He spoke firmly. "Yes, yes, their file has been closed and all charges dropped."

Shaun who spoke first. "What, you mean—?" I cut him off. "You mean we are free to go?" Our probation officer nodded her head confidently that yes, we were free to go. Shaun said, "You mean we don't have to go into court today?" The Crown Attorney confidently answered, "You do not have to attend today's court, but you can if you want, and have the judge confirm what I have already conveyed, but need I remind you your last name starts with R and you will wait most of the day!" We all laughed at his comment.

Shaun and I were ecstatic and again were not expecting this blessing. I shook both the attorney's hand and our probation officer's hand. I may even have given her a hug. I couldn't contain my spiritual delight and all the while was saying loudly, "Oh, thank you, Jesus! Thank you, God! What an amazing miracle! I'm not a criminal. Thank you, Jesus!" I made it very clear to them the fear I had felt over the fact that my nursing licence would have been affected. I was on my second round of handshakes and had seen a smile cross the attorney's face. When I shook his hand the second time, he clasped his other hand over top and in a strong confirming voice said to me, "Go and sin no more!" He now was grinning from ear to ear, as was I. Oh, I loved it! It was an amazing confirmation for me to have this Crown Attorney use one of Jesus' most famous lines, one he often used after performing a miracle.

I had seen Jesus in the gym, in the CFS office and now I saw him in the court office! Praise be to God, hallelujah! Shaun and I floated out of the court office. I love this part of our story! God had put all the right people in our path to make us successful in this most difficult season.

The Rumancik Crew could now begin the long journey back to healing. It would be a long road as our foundation had been broken but we trusted that God was going to make a stronger one. We worked hard at incorporating the lessons that we had learned and made it a mission to shower Bailey with grace and love. I had asked Bailey in the beginning to admit that he had gone too far in all he said, and he readily agreed. We kept our vows to him and surrounded our children with protective love.

The trauma that we went through had many ripple effects. As I read in a journal entry dated around this time, it was clear how I was still struggling with some strongholds. During a church service where our minister was giving a short drama presentation, he made it clear that God who created us in His image did indeed create the emotion of anger. He described anger as a gift that you could purchase at God's emotional store. But, he said, the warning on the label of the box of anger warned that this emotion was intended for good and not evil, for motivation not destruction and if you didn't watch this emotion closely it could turn into a monster and take over your home, thus destroying the members of your family in its wake.

The end of this drama presentation was one filled with grace. He made it clear that God's store of emotions had an amazing exchange policy, and that if you found that you had purchased this emotion and had now found that it was destroying you and your family, then you could simply exchange the box of anger for another emotion. You could ask God to replace it with something else that would nurture your home and help those within your home thrive.

Needless to say, my loving husband was sending enough elbow nudges my way to make it clear that he thought this was about me. I was irritated and annoyed but knew I couldn't argue the point.

After the sermon was over and our minister had given a personal testimony on anger, there was an opportunity at the front of the church for prayer support. I grabbed my pride and left the pew where I was sitting with my husband. I would see what God could do with my anger issue. As I stood in front of the church and began to confess my sorrows to the couple standing in front of me, I quickly included all that we had just been through and how I was struggling with the anger monster in my life.

My husband came up behind me, wrapped his arms around me, cut me off mid-sentence and summed up my struggle confidently in one statement, "My wife has purchased the box of anger and she doesn't want to give it up!"

I was annoyed and immediately began to protest but I soon had to give up when I realized he was completely right. I loved anger—it had been part of my life since I was a little girl, and to me anger was both a safe place and home. How would I ever give up my friend, anger? It had always been there for me and had helped me get through some of my most difficult seasons? It was then that I was counselled in a godly way that my anger could be returned to God and He would return to me another emotion that would help build a healthy home instead of destruction. I felt a burning in my stomach as I began to struggle with the thought of giving up my long-time companion, anger. It would be a long process to return my purchase to God and I knew that what I wanted instead was peace and freedom. I would never be able to be used by God in my destiny if I didn't release my anger and its sidekick, bad words. I don't think any of us would have been surprised to know that it would take almost four years to journey through the healing process.

During those first few months, we were still pursuing our move closer to family. Shaun and I had decided he would not take the job opportunity that he had at the beginning of our ordeal but a friend of Shaun's had taken a job in the potash industry in Saskatchewan and we decided that he too would apply. Within twenty-four hours he had a call for a job interview and we were thrilled.

Within no time at all, Shaun was hired and employed at the potash mine and our days were busy in preparation for the sale of our home and the prospect of a new one. Shaun began his new job training. We had made many many trips from Cold Lake to Portage so I was very well aware of the towns that were near the TransCanada Highway known as the Yellowhead. We began to explore possible locations to settle, and I was eager to be working in a province that acknowledged the role of a licensed practical nurse to its full scope of practice. I had heard a lot of good things about these job perspectives. It also made me proud that I could say I had been employed as a nurse in Manitoba, Alberta and Saskatchewan.

I decided to phone one of the local hospitals and enquire about a few things. Once on the phone with a nurse, I quickly had all of my questions met. I enjoyed my conversation with this stranger as she was very friendly. I ended my conversation with the question, "Are there any nurses who love Jesus?" She very quickly told me that I would get along great with a nurse by the name of Pat. (I would meet this nurse and she would become one of my dearest friends, cheering me on as I discover what Christ has planned for me.) I was thankful they humoured me in my passion for Jesus. I had taken my faith walk very seriously and looked for any opportunity to pray with my patients. I would never push my faith on anyone but would simply pray this prayer before my feet walked onto the hospital wards: "Lord Jesus, I will walk through any doors You want me to walk through. Please guide me and direct me to do Your will." I had made some awesome memories praying for the people who were in my care and still practice this tradition very seriously.

I was going to miss my coworkers very much as they had all become close friends and had been an incredible support all the times I had found myself reorienting back to work after a maternity leave. I had once heard one of them call me "Jesus Jenny" and my first thought was that they were poking fun at me. It was my friend Jen who looked at me sheepishly as if caught with a hidden secret. She reassured me very quickly that they meant no harm by it. I was worried that they thought I was a religious freak and very quickly realized that they had identified Jesus in me. I had shown them I had my faith at the centre of my life, and I tucked this compliment into my heart and cherished my nickname given to me by my nursing buddies. I knew that they were well aware that I hated religion but was very much for a relationship with Jesus.

Shaun and I decided that we would not take the opportunity to rent relocation housing that the potash mines were offering but instead purchase our very own fifth-wheel trailer. I would stay behind and let our school-aged kids finish up the school year, then we would join Shaun for the summer holidays. It was difficult to be apart from Shaun, but I enjoyed his evening calls.

The kids and I tried our best to make the most of our time alone. My sister who was always ready for an adventure thought it would be a great opportunity to take her very active nephew Glen Lawrence to his first movie theatre experience. We soon made it a full family affair, with Bailey and his friend going to see the new *A-Team* movie and the rest of us (along with Anna's friend Vickie) going to see the new and awaited *Toy Story* movie. Glen's eyes were as big as saucers as he took in the sounds and sights of the large screen before us. Within a few moments we soon saw our beloved Buzz Lightyear. The theatre was completely silent as we waited for the first opening lines, long enough of a silence to hear our Glen Lawrence yell enthusiastically, "Hey, Buzz – it's me, Glen! Hi Buzz! Buzz, it's me!" The whole theatre erupted in laughter and none was more amused than the row of college students who looked back at Glen and said, "Dude, that's awesome!"

When school was out, we were on our way to see Shaun. I decided to leave a few days earlier than planned, as we wanted to surprise Shaun at the end of his day of work. I loved the kids' enthusiasm as we parked at the mine's visitors parking lot. Daddy was going to be so surprised. When we spotted Shaun leaving work with a long line of co-workers, their conversations were all interrupted with kids screaming, "Daddy, Daddy!" The look on Shaun's face was priceless; we had truly surprised him. All the other workers smiled at the happy reunion.

The first person to welcome us to Langenburg was a kind post office attendant who helped me find various moms groups around the town. Then, while we were camping in the Churchbridge campground, a kind lady approached us and invited us to attend a Vacation Bible School that coming week. I was delighted to attend. The kids and I made ready for the fun summer event and were greeted warmly by the Lutheran congregation. It would be the first of many church denominations that I would get to know. I loved the worship and felt my spirit filled with the anointed tunes. Our kids quickly got involved in the worship service. Bailey was in Portage for the summer holidays so it was a nice outlet for the younger Rumancik crew.

Glen had his own way of doing everything and at the age of three he was very well on his way to prove to the world that he did not need Mommy's guidance. He proved this on the second day of their VBS week. Glen was very stubborn when it came to his attire and he loved when he discovered that certain summer shorts had a built-in lining—to him, you didn't need to wear underwear with such shorts. We had constant conversations about the fact that he still did have to wear underwear.

On day two of VBS, the kind woman who had invited us to come was all smiles as she was told me how Glen's shorts had given way during worship. He had been at the front of the church and enjoying the action-packed tune that they were practicing. She said his hands had been raised and he was singing to Jesus when his shorts dropped to the floor. He didn't miss a beat and had no care in the world as she readjusted his shorts around his little waist. I thanked Miriam kindly as I sat and watched the kids finish up their activities.

I was on my way out of the church when suddenly a panicked thought crossed my mind. I hoped to God that Glen had remembered my clear instructions that morning to put on his underpants. I quickly stopped Glen to inspect his shorts and gasped when I saw that he was naked as a jaybird underneath, which meant that he had been buck naked worshipping Jesus at the front of the Lutheran church.

I quickly found Miriam and she very quickly confirmed my fears: "Yup, and he had no care in the world and he just kept right on singing." I then proceeded to find the minister who had been in attendance during the session. I apologized and he said, "Don't worry—it happens all the time." I know he was just trying to reassure my embarrassed state but I couldn't help but say, "You mean this sort of thing happens all the time during your worship services?" and to this we both had a very big laugh.

I will forever be thankful for the invitation to join in on the Vacation Bible School. We also enjoyed similar events in the town of Langenburg. The towns were seven minutes apart and we spent much time in both.

One of my favourite stories about our transition from Manitoba to Alberta to Saskatchewan had to do with our routine of taking recycling into Langenburg while our laundry dried at the laundromat in Churchbridge. On one of these excursions we were met with some stern looks as we brought in our empty water bottles. The attendant looked out at our vehicle and asked where we were from. I was in a joking mood and said we were from Alberta. That answer seemed to bring this attendant great stress. She made it very clear that it was illegal to bring other recyclables into the province from another province. I quickly informed her that we were indeed staying in the Churchbridge campground for some of the summer weeks; she still looked at me with skepticism as she dealt with my recyclables.

The next trip we made, she still wanted more proof that I indeed was moving to Saskatchewan. I didn't realize how much my licence plates messed with her. In Alberta it was not mandatory to have provincial plates on the front of your van so Shaun and I had decided to leave our Manitoba licence plates on the front of our vehicles and have the legal plates stating that we resided in the province of Alberta on the back. So this stern lady thought I was a complete liar.

She also told me that there was a lot of bootlegging. Under the impression that bootlegging was the involvement of illegal selling of alcohol, I was shocked that she thought I looked like a woman who would bootleg from one province to another. I asked her what exactly her definition of bootlegging was. It also meant bringing recycling and other goods from out of province to redeem them, selling produce and poultry across provincial lines, etc. I gasped and, without thinking, said out loud, "My grandfather was a bootlegger!?!" I couldn't believe that all those years my grandfather could have worn the title as bootlegger of recyclable goods. I still chuckle at her next reaction. She was stunned—just when she thought she could trust me, here I was confessing that I was born from a long line of bootleggers. The attendant's co-worker looked on, smiling with amusement but the first attendant assured me that he could be fined a large amount if he was ever caught. With a great big smile on behalf of my beloved Grandpa, I said, "Nope, you'll never get him—he's in heaven with Jesus!" These two attendants and I are still close and I love teasing them that they once thought I was a bootlegger.

Many of us can relate to the trials involved in relocations, especially when your plans do not play out as you hoped. As Shaun left for work one morning, he kissed me on the cheek and told me and the kids to find a home. With a hubby releasing me on a mission like this one, I was determined to find us a home, and off we went. Our travels led us to Langenburg where I took note of a property and phoned the realtor's number on the sign. As I called, a pleasant voice confirmed that the property that I was looking at had already been sold and had been one of many that had been listed and sold within a twenty-four-hour period. Yes, that was definitely a reality that Shaun and I were very well aware of.

The realtor was determined to find us a home and I appreciated her enthusiastic personality. As she gave me the directions to another property, I was soon on my way and parked in front of the property, my mouth dropping open. My spirit leaped and I felt that this was our perfect home. I felt I heard the Lord say that this was the property for us to continue our rest and healing. I just had to convince my husband that this was the right home. Hadn't he kissed me on the cheek that very morning and released me to find us a home? I confidently prepared myself to inform him that I was the type of girl who got the job done!

Let's just say that my husband wasn't all that thrilled with the find. He just had so much convinced himself that we had moved to Saskatchewan to finally be able to buy a farm and this wasn't it. I was in a trusting-God mode and felt very strongly that we were to purchase this home. We would wait and see.

While I waited, I was beginning to feel the toll of the loneliness creep in that I would no longer have the strong friend base I had had in Cold Lake. We had had many Christian friends and had made a lot of memories with them. How would I be able to let this go and find true friends in these small towns? I did not know it but God was about to give me the greatest friend I would ever need. We had been to a few churches in the area and looked first for a Pentecostal church. We had attended a Sunday morning service and had been engulfed by warmth and love. It was during our Sunday morning visit to the Pentecostal church that my greatest friend would find me.

The day after I had mourned and prayed about leaving my old friends behind and asking the Lord to send me new friends, a Suburban pulled up to our campsite and a stunning woman climbed out and greeted me warmly. She carried a gift of homemade buns and gushed with enthusiasm as she met me. Her introduction was this: "Hi, my name is Cindy and I hear you love the Lord." I loved her greeting and was quickly in awe of my answer to prayer—not that I would ever want to replace my friend Cindy in Cold Lake but was thrilled at God's confirmation that he had found me a Jesus girl and she was also named Cindy. She told me much about the women's ministry at their church and the Bible study group starting soon. I was over the moon with joy. Jesus had heard me and given me all that I would ever need in Christian sisters. Soon I was visited by the pastor's wife from the Langenburg church. As Donna came to our campsite, she spoke to my daughter Sadie and said cheerfully, "Would you like some vegetables from my garden?" Never being keen on veggies, Sadie didn't miss a beat and confidently answered, "No thanks!" I clarified very quickly that we would be thankful to receive her blessed garden goodies. Donna then presented the kids with some cassette tapes as she thought our camper would have a cassette deck. I was so thankful for the evening entertainment it would bring.

A few weeks into September we moved into our new home. I was thrilled and so were the kids, but my hubby was not so happy and made it very noticeable that this was not his plan. It would be the beginning of our hardest years of marriage as time would reveal how much Shaun had not dealt with in our Cold Lake season. Who could blame him for the trauma that still was taking its toll?

The damage that a family goes through after an ordeal like ours is something you can only realize if you've gone through it. You wonder if any bad morning will bring about these horrific events again. You wonder if you're a good enough mother or father. You wonder what form of discipline is crossing the line. How often had we both witnessed and heard of families making the same mistakes as we had, and we wondered why they didn't have an intervention like ours. Our family was no different than anyone elses but we were always on high alert and trying very much to survive each day.

The school systems in the area became our family's biggest allies. There were many times they advocated on our behalf and recognized the tenderness of our rebuilding years. The guidance counselor was someone who was a gift and we felt it divine appointment the times she played a role in intervening during difficult seasons. We were so thankful that our new elementary school was just beginning to have a government-approved Pre-K program, which proved to be a perfect outlet for our very active Glen. We were settling into our new adventure with Sadie in grade one and Bailey in grade ten, Glen entering Pre-K, and Emma home with Mom. I was so thankful for our kind-hearted elementary school principal, Mr. Kirk, who was there for our family on our most difficult days.

18 LEARNING TO LOVE AND TRUST GOD MORE

OUR NEW ADVENTURE WOULD PROVE THAT MUCH HEALING WAS ON ITS WAY AND WE as a family were covered with much blessing. My husband's discerning spirit felt led to have our family join in on a small and cozy church. I did not agree with his choice but in obedience decided to trust him. I shudder at how different our lives would be had we not made this sweet congregation our church family. My submission to my husband in this season proved that I would stand by him and trust his wisdom even when I thought he couldn't possibly be making the right choice. It would prove that God's ways are so much bigger than we can ever dare imagine. In this church I would find the most vibrant and authentic woman you could ever find. My friend Melisa, the pastor's wife, would be my biggest advocate in my vulnerable healing journey. Her authentic nature is truly a gift and she uses it to spread the truth of God's genuine love and grace at the Church of God. Her husband, our kind-hearted pastor Aaron, would become one of my husband's most treasured friends. This couple would be fundamental in aiding in our family's destiny. Aaron longed to mould and mentor those chosen by God, and I am so thankful that he believed that God had begun a great gift within me.

With this congregation also came a church camp. I very quickly took on the role as camp nurse and with it came many awesome opportunities to grow in faith. During Squirt Camp came an open door that I would have never seen coming. One day, I sent the chapel speaker to the hospital with a potentially serious symptom, leaving a vacancy in the kids chapel. I very eagerly volunteered to help by teaching the Bible stories as I had grown to love. I had so much fun and could never have done it without the love and support of the camp staff, especially my wardrobe and makeup artist, my friend Melisa. I will never forget how much fun we had that summer and her confidence in my ability to stretch my horizons from Sunday School teacher to chapel speaker. Who could also ever forget our hilarious attempts to get up on the water trampoline in the lake? God was amazing and at the end of summer I became highly recommended and have been kids camp chapel speaker ever since. I would have never had that opportunity had I not honoured my husband's vision for attending the right congregation just for us. I am so thankful for the mentorship of our church.

My friend Cindy would introduce me to many women who were beautiful inside and out. From the very beginning of our move to Saskatchewan, I would sit around a Bible study table that was filled with ladies who represented more than one denomination. We would all sit and learn about the greatness of God and his wonderful word as one joint group. I am so thankful that I met my sweet friend Carolyne who would teach me much about the Catholic faith and that there were Spirit-filled believers in any denomination. Shaun and I grew to love both her and her hubby Dennis. As my husband put it, we would attend the Langenburg Fellowship during the week and worship in Churchbridge on Sunday. In five years this has still remained our mission and I have enjoyed growing in my faith with the women's ministry group in Langenburg and the warmth and support of our congregation in the town of Churchbridge. Both congregations have been a big part of our church family.

Trying to balance all of life can be a big struggle and even greater a battle when there are underlying stresses. One particular day, I was pleading with God to please help me figure out how to end the ongoing struggle with my emotional rollercoaster. Something just didn't seem right and I could see all kinds of moms living with harmony all around me. I prayed specifically as the tears were streaming down my face, "Please God, help me figure out what is going on with my body right down to the cellular level." My answer to prayer soon came when the phone rang. It was my friend Cindy, my spiritual sister. We had grown so close since I moved to Langenburg and I was so thankful to have a friend who shared my passionate faith. After I had explained to her that I just couldn't seem to shake this weariness, she encouraged me to have my blood analyzed by a biochemist she had been seeing for years. I took this opportunity and found life-changing truths about what I had been struggling with for all my life. I truly had my prayers answered by God—down to the cellular level.

I was thankful that my husband had his own dose of stress and had now learned to sympathize with me. The onset of shift work had given my husband his fair share of unstable moods. All those years when he thought I was just some kind of angry crazy lady when coming off night shifts, and now he knew the emotional ups and downs that come from sleepless nights due to work

We also finally had neighbours we could call friends, people that we would grow to love and cherish. When Kristy first saw me waving at her through her dining window, her first thought was "crazy lady", but she and her husband Justin soon discovered that Shaun and I were to be commited friends who would all too well understand all the trials life could throw at any family. She has become a treasured friend who has taught me much about homesteading.

Through these newfound friends we would find our dream property. God had placed us in the right home for such a time as this, as the writer of Esther would say. We had prayed and believed that a farm would come our way and two years to the date that we moved in to Langenburg, we moved onto our acreage. Our home in Langenburg selling in just three days, God made it clear that indeed the doors were blown wide open. As my husband walked around his new property, he stated in awe, "I never believed that God could take the picturesque ideal farm I had envisioned in my mind for so long and make it happen." We rejoiced as a family and continued our growth in Christ.

God uses all things in our lives to bring forth his plan and purpose in our lives. A friendship that grows from a first greeting becomes exactly what you need at one of your darkest moments. No friendship proved this more than my friendship with Lorraine. When Bailey started dating, he threw all of life's goals to the side, including his academic prospect of graduation. I would learn much from my relationship with this girl, Amanda, who would eventually bring us our first grandchild, our sweet Aubree Dawn. I definitely struggled with giving up on my ideals for my son. I had dreamed of the day that he would graduate and I could sever the strings and let him go. This, of course, was not what life would allow, and once again a teenager proved he would know best and fly the coop sooner than expected. I had to die to these dreams for my son, and it was my sweet friend Lorraine who sat with me and helped me through the mom emotions. It is so extraordinary how God places all the right friendships into your path.

I soon realized that I had never lived in a small community like this and then heard Jesus clearly confirm that He had done it on purpose. He moved a girl named Jenny so full of Jesus' light and said, "I release you in the light of Christ to love." I couldn't help it if I tried for it was brimming out of me and I am so thankful for my training ground and all those I have gotten to bless. Thanks for letting me in!

We sometimes try to figure out how God is going to change a circumstance but can never see how vast His ways are. I would have never guessed that in a million years that it would be a quiet widow who would bring me such a message of hope. Her marriage ended in a tragedy, after they had only been married for a few years. It was her shy but courageous voice that would affirm the need for healing intervention in marriage. My cherished friend Diane encouraged Shaun and me to partake in a seminar called Choices that would be life-changing and the most amazing experience we would both have for complete emotional healing.

This seminar would be where I would finally realize how much I had trapped that little girl whose brother had died deep inside my soul. I could not seem to come to terms with my struggle with freedom. It was a life coach who looked at me and blasted a truth directly into my inner prison. She spoke honestly and gently, saying, "Jenny, what's it going to take for you to let that little girl out to play again?" I sat stunned as she spoke that truth to me and then felt the heat begin to erupt in my inner core. Within moments I saw a vision of me as a small little girl hiding in the hallway outside my parents' bedroom, my father on the bed covered in my brother's blood and the deep wailing that came from both my parents. I recalled a voice clearly reinforcing to my whole being, "It's over—you have to grow up now, no more silliness, no more just worrying about fun. You have to be a big girl, a bigger helper." This had been the vow that I enclosed around my precious spirit, entrapping my youthful innocence. I knew that that moment was where my freedom to be fun-loving had been taken and stolen. I was astonished to realize that this was how it had all began. All those years where I struggled to push that inner child away and then keep her locked up. All the times where I found I couldn't release the freedom to just let my children be fun-loving kids. Always trying to keep order and to control and reinforce the silliness that children naturally possess. I declared a new contract loud and proud: "I am a free and courageous woman!" The little girl inside me has been nourished and protected as precious ever since.

Another healing point in the Choices seminar happened as I had another recollection of my childhood that I had all but forgotten. I had forgotten my Uncle Steve who would release my spirit to fly. He noticed my withdrawn nature and acknowledged that I also had an ability to run like the wind. He would encourage me on many summer evenings to run a race against anyone. I was so pleased to race and run and feel the speed and the freedom as the wind whipped at the loose strands of my hair. He would cheer me on in my every win, and challenge any kid that happened to be visiting to dare to take on his champ. I felt the powerful release in how it felt to excel in all those races while letting my light shine for Uncle Steve, my running coach and whomever else was nearby. Was it a small coincidence that this same uncle was there to cut me a cheque during my passing grades in nursing college? I think not. I decided at the end of the seminar that I would love nothing more than to light people's way to run the race that Jesus has set for every one of us to run. There is great success in finding your own personal relationship with Jesus as your spiritual trainer.

Finally I had the freedom to be myself and to not hide my light away from the world. It was clear that as a little girl I had made a commitment to a Scripture verse and now I had a declaration all brand new: *"Let your light so shine before men, that they may see your good works, and glorify your Father which is in heaven"* (Matthew 5:16, KJV).

I had met Jesus at the gym and realized that only in a relationship with Him could there be true healing and restoration. Jesus is in the restoration business. I can't imagine how people try and live their lives without the greatest personal trainer that ever lived. Jesus Christ, my best friend, my coach through every life struggle. Through my journey with my best friend I know that I will truly find my destiny, the one that He alone has for me, I have a new understanding of the anointing of Queen Esther. She was brave and courageous. I wish to use this bravery and courage and use it to tell the world about Jesus Christ the one who met me at the gym in the early hours of my sorrow and who continues to meet with me every day.

THE HUTTERITES

For as long as I can remember there have been many questions about my former culture. Some questions and comments were a joy to answer but others were filled with ignorance that cut deep into my heart. It is very important for me that this writing project include as much information about the Hutterites as possible. In the following pages you will be given a sneak peek into the writings found on the Hutterite Brethren website. I would like to encourage all my readers to please seek out all of your unanswered questions. This website is beautifully displayed and very informative. The pictures on the site give a generous look into the culture that will always be dear to my heart.

(Information about the Hutterites here and throughout the book is taken with permission from the Hutterite Brethren website: http://www.hutterites.org/)

HUTTERITES, MENNONITES (AND THUS AMISH WHO ARE OF MENNONITE DESCENT) SHARE common roots. These groups are Anabaptists, and these movements trace their history back to the Reformation. Anabaptists believe in adult baptism, choosing to follow in the steps of the Lord Jesus Christ who was baptized as an adult.

The Hutterite religion is unique in that they believe in community of goods, with all material goods held in common. This idea is gleaned from several biblical sources. We read that Jesus and his disciples shared everything. John 4:12 states that the disciples shared a common purse. In Matthew 19, Jesus explained to the rich young ruler that he needed to follow the commandments, to give all he had to the poor and to follow him. Throughout the gospels, we see that Christ teaches us to love our neighbours, and the manifestation of this love can be seen is in caring for each other and in the sharing of possessions. The apostles and the early Christians held all things in common (Acts 2:44-47, Acts 4:32-35). The Hutterites believe the community of goods and working for each other to be ways of obeying the command of love. All members of the colony are provided for equally and no assets are to be kept for personal gain. Hutterites do not have personal bank accounts; all earnings are held communally, and necessities are distributed according to need. Hutterites believe that all their work is to benefit the community and is a form of service to God. They work for each other; however, instead of wages all necessities of life are provided. Each member serves the other through their work and labour.

Hutterites have a detailed record of their history dating back to the beginning of their story. These chronicles contain inspiring stories of faithfulness, doctrinal statements and exhortations on biblical texts. These texts and exhortations are also known as teachings (or *Lehren)*, and are included in all worship services. Together these documents represent a rich literary tradition that Hutterites today draw from to guide their living.

Since the early sixteenth century, this Anabaptist sect has endured great persecution and death at the hands of both the state and church in medieval Europe. However the hand of God remained constant with these people and their descendants survive to this day.

Hutterite history involves a succession of migration in search of religious freedom. Over a period of four-and-a-half centuries, they moved from Germany and Austria (Czech Republic) to Hungary and farther south to Transylvania (which today is Romania), then north to Kiev in Ukraine, south to the Molotschna in Ukraine near Alexandrovsk, Zaporozhie, across the Atlantic to the Dakotas in the USA and finally during World War I, up to the Canadian Prairies

The Hutterite move to America from Russia came after Russia began making it compulsory for everyone to join the military. Also all citizens were to be taught the Russian language. Consequently, on April 14, 1873, two Hutterite men (Paul and Lorenz Tschetter) set out for United States of America in search of suitable land. During WWI, the United States government passed the Selective Service Act, which meant that all young men aged 21-31 were conscripted into the army. Hutterites ran into difficulty when they requested exemption from military work orders and military uniforms. They even met with the President of the United States, Ulysses S. Grant, to ask him to grant them military exception, but he was unable to secure this. At this time, though, the Canadian government still needed settlers on the prairies. They welcomed the Hutterites, assuring them their religious freedom and exemption from military services. In 1918, therefore, the Hutterites immigrated to Canada.

There are three different (distinct) Hutterites groups: the Schmiedleut group was named after Michael Waldner who was a blacksmith and was called Schmied-michel, because the German word for smith is Schmied. Darius Walter's group called Dariusleut. The third and final group that left Russia was led by Jacob Wipf, a teacher. Since the German word for teacher is Lehrer, his group is known as Lehrerleut.

In a vision, an angel showed Michael Waldner the ethereal beauty of heaven and the agony of hell. When Waldner asked the angel where his assigned place was, the angel reminded him that in the great flood only the eight persons inside the ark were saved. The angel went on to admonish him that the ark symbolized the *Gemeinscsft*, communion of the Holy Spirit, and instructed him to re-establish community in the manner of Jesus and his disciples. Waking from his trance, Waldner was surprised to find his family (who had taken him for dead) weeping by his bedside. Thereafter, he and another minister worked hard to establish a community as such.

A Hutterite minister once claimed that in order for Hutterites to survive, they must at all cost and in all ways possible remain totally separated from the world. He lamented the growing influence that off-colony visits were having on his colony members. Other Hutterite leaders claim that, while uninterrupted interactions with the world may not be desirable, it is impossible to totally isolate members, and attempting to do so may induce them to leave. They espouse a strategy of convincing members that living in a Hutterite colony is the best way to serve God and to follow Christ's commands to love neighbour as self. Both of these views enjoy a substantial following by various colony members throughout North America.

Hutterites try to be true to their understanding of the Gospel. They are New Testament people. They try to live by the ideal of the Sermon on the Mount.

One of the Hutterites' earliest proverbs is translated: "Community and fellowship wouldn't be hard, if self-seeking were not there."

It is important to remember that Hutterite communities are very diverse and that no two communities are identical in their organization and overall way of life. There are, however, some characteristics that are similar in most communities. In every colony, the minister is both the spiritual leader and the chief executor. He is also part of an advisory board that makes day-to-day decisions affecting the community. The advisory board consists of the colony manager, the farm manager, and two or three witness brothers or deacons. The colony manager receives and pays the bills, does the banking and is the business manager of the colony. The numerous activities of each colony are managed by witness brothers (deacons) or other brothers.

Since their Anabaptist beginnings in sixteenth-century Europe, Hutterites have practiced both a modest and simple uniform dress code. The early traditional style originates from the German and Austrian national costume. For the men and boys, black lederhosen and suspenders are worn. The dirndl, a sleeveless dress with a blouse and an apron, is worn by the woman and girls. Over the years, Hutterites have made modifications to make them more serviceable and comfortable. In addition to its value as a cultural tradition this outward symbol of unity and modesty is an integral part of their faith life, identifying and reminding them who they are as a people.

Most colonies are sustained through farming as a livelihood. Most colonies grow crops and manage fair-sized farms of between 3000-12000 acres, depending on the area. Hutterites also raise a large amount of livestock, in some cases producing up to thirty percent of a state or province's hogs, eggs or turkeys. Hutterites colonies are self-sufficient, raising most of the food that is consumed including broilers, geese and ducks.

In addition to agriculture, manufacturing has been gaining a solid foothold on more and more colonies. Diversification into manufacturing is becoming more important for several reasons. The use of modern technology and large machinery has resulted in fewer workers being required for crop production. In addition, excessive capital cost associated with the new land purchases or new barn construction has also been an obstacle in expanding farms. As a result, more colonies have invested in manufacturing as a means of supplementing their income.

Between fifty and 120 people typically live on a Hutterite colony. The colony size is often about eighty people from approximately fourteen families.

Women serve many roles in the community. A married woman is responsible for various housekeeping duties such as sewing, cleaning, and caring for her family. Women also manages community duties such as cooking, baking, gardening, and food preservation. A female head cook works with several rotating pairs of married and single woman who assist her on a weekly basis.

Families take turns using the communal laundromat. Industrial dryers are available as well, but because nothing compares to the crisp, fresh scent of air dried laundry, women prefer to let the sun dry their family's homemade shirts, dresses, and blouses.

In addition to regular schooling, children attend German school where they learn to read and write in standard German. This class is typically before and after regular school hours on weekdays. Hutterites actually speak three languages: Hutterisch, German and English.

Church services, which are held daily on most communities, form the core of Hutterite devotional life. They serve to refocus life on God. Evening services, known as *Gebet*, are approximately half an hour in length, and take place before the evening meal. On Sunday and on holy days, church is held in the forenoon as well. The morning service typically lasts about seventy-five minutes.

Easter is an important time for most Hutterite young people with many of them deciding to get baptized at Easter. Baptism, or *Tauffest*, is one of the most important steps in the life of a Hutterite. Once someone is baptized, they are considered full members of the Hutterite church. Hutterites accept all twelve points of the Apostle's Creed upon baptism. Easter holidays last four days. Hutterites partake in communion only once a year, during the sacred Easter holiday.

Contact Jenny Rumancik

If you would like to schedule an interview
or speaking engagement with Jenny Rumancik,
please contact her at

jrum2911@gmail.com